ADVENTURES WITH COWBOY BOB

Fun Tales About Country Life

R.E. Beebe
&
J.M. Marsing

Cover design by Judith S. Design & Creativity
www.judithsdesign.com
Published by Glass Spider Publishing
www.glassspiderpublishing.com

DEDICATION

This book is lovingly dedicated to Bob Marsing. Bob shared with us his love of cowboy ways, horses, the Utah desert, and history. Family was all important to him. He is greatly missed by all who knew him.

J.M. Marsing

To Bob, whose attitude about life, and ready laughter, changed all of us. And to Mom, without whose assistance this book could not have been written. She embraced Bob's hobbies, interests, and especially family, as if they were her own. We learned to have a curiosity about all things, and what it means to love, from her.

R.E. Beebe

FOREWORD

This book was a long time in the making. Three of the stories in it were written when I was in my early twenties. Then I decided, more than ten years ago, to create a book from the various stories our family likes to tell. I had no idea it would take so long to put it together. Writing about true events takes a lot more research, discussion, and editing than writing fiction. As a result, although I'd started turning this into a book seven years before I began the *Sylvio* series, six of those books were published before this one even went to the editor. Fiction, at least for me, is much easier to put on paper.

As I researched the backgrounds and scenes for this book, I found it fascinating listening to different versions of the same story. People will swear their version is correct and that the other people who were there have it wrong. It made me appreciate what cops, reporters, and lawyers must experience when they interview people while trying to discern the truth.

I am very grateful to family members and friends for sharing their memories and thoughts, and for being willing to let me publish the stories. Some of the names have been changed, usually because I could not locate the person after so many years. And some names had been forgotten entirely by those involved.

Often what those involved think is ordinary life is viewed quite differently after time. I'm sure Bob's parents, June and Edith, did not think their diaries would be interesting to anyone else, but they were an invaluable source of information. They were a fascinating insight into what, from my perspective, was a harsh and demanding life, and was simply living for them.

Books are not written alone. I want to thank my friends and family who read the rough drafts and helped improve them. And I especially want to thank the critters who, like Bob, brought laughter and joy to everyday life. As with all of my books, any mistakes in this one are mine.

Sit back and enjoy this brief escape from the mundane.

PROLOGUE: THE STORY BEHIND THE STORIES

Bob was born in a small house in Wellington, Utah, on February 12, 1930. He was christened Robert Wayne Marsing. Others would say his childhood was not an easy one; that the family lived in poverty and didn't settle in one place to build any roots. Bob never saw it that way. He viewed living with his own brand of *joie de vivre*. Everyday life, for Bob, was a chance to find something to laugh about. He always had a story to tell and had a knack for seeing even the most normal things in a humorous light. As I've gotten older, I have realized how rare an individual he was. It is an unusual gift to spread joy wherever you go.

This book is a collection of his stories and other fun things that seem to happen whenever animals (a.k.a. critters) are involved. I don't have Bob's talent for putting as much humor into the stories as he could, but I'll do my best to do his stories justice.

Bob and the majority of our family members speak "country." I'll try to add translations to things that might seem a little strange to those who aren't from our part of the country, or who don't live on a farm.

Enjoy!

Newlyweds Bob and Joyce Marsing. Syracuse, Utah. January 1980.

PART ONE:
THE GOOD OLD DAYS

ROUGHIN' IT

Bob's dad, June, was raised on a large ranch in central Utah. The ranch comes into this collection of stories a little later. June's love of living on the Red Cliff Ranch and exploring the wild country of central and southern Utah never left him. He spent most of his life wandering the desert and was never content to settle in one place. As a result, Bob had called fifty-two places home by his 50th year, and attended twelve schools by the time he was in the eighth grade. Some of those homes were nothing more than wall tents (canvas tents with plywood walls on the inside). Bob quit school to work full time after eighth grade. He got his GED while serving in the Army.

Most of us these days live in ease and comfort, at least in our part of the world. Our biggest worry in the morning is whether the coffee pot will work and if our phone is charged. Things were quite a bit different for June and Edith, who were a young couple raising a growing family during the depression years. Making a living was tough for almost anyone in the 1930s. Choosing to do it in that beautiful but barren part of Utah was harder still.

It's easy to forget how much antibiotics and vaccines have altered our everyday lives. Until ready access to such gifts, it was quite common for one or more children in a family to die of disease or infection. Most families lived through the loss of children, and June's family was no exception.

June and Edith had six children. The first five were each about a year and a half apart. Norma was the oldest. She lived to be ninety-four and was one day short of her seventy-fifth wedding anniversary when she passed. She was followed by Rosalee, who was almost six when she died of an infection of the mastoid. After her was Junie, who was named after her father, and who lived to be eighty-six. Bob was next. He was the only boy and lived to be one month short of eighty-three. Lois followed Bob. She died of meningitis when she was not quite six. Sherma, the last of the children, was a surprise baby. She was thirteen years younger than Bob, and she missed out on most of the family travels.

At the Cat Ranch. From left: June, Bob, Edith, Norma, Lois,
a family friend, Rosalee, and Junie.

Bob lost the son he named after himself to cardiac arrest caused by cancer when Bobby was almost twelve. Another son, christened Timothy, died as a result of being born premature. Bob's other two children, Jessie and David, come into these stories a few times themselves. They both have Bob's sense of humor and spread their own brand of joy to those who know them.

Disease and infection were not the only dangers June's family faced. Bob's mother, Edith, instilled a fear of snakes in her children that none of them ever lost. We teased Bob about it a lot when we got the chance. But Edith had good reasons for training her kids that way. Living as they did, it was a common thing for families to lose some, if not all, of their children to hardship, accident, or disease. Her children were not allowed to swim in the river or go near a snake, since they lived too far from town to get medical help in time.

People complain about inconveniences today. Life can be hard, but we have a different perspective than those who were scratching a living farming wild country with no ready access to doctors, police, or even close neighbors.

Most of the time, they lived out on the desert, but when Edith was ready to deliver a child, June brought the family to town so she would be with midwives who could assist with the births. When Bob was due to be born, Rosalee and Junie stayed at their Aunt Effie's house, and Norma stayed with her mom to help the older women. Bob grew up to look like a mirror image of his dad, but when he was born, Norma said he "looked like a little red monkey." Bob wasn't the only one in the family with a sense of humor.

Bob had a knack for thinking outside of the box, sort of like Dr. Seuss. He viewed the things people and animals did from a slightly different angle. He seemed to have inherited that ability. His great-grandfather invented the name Marsing. Apparently, he got tired of there being so many families named Larsen. Today, there are enough Marsings wandering the country that there is even a town in Idaho named for Bob's uncles.

With that said, let us begin with some of the stories about Bob's parents and his life as a boy.

THE POND

When there are emergencies, many people freeze in place. They can't seem to think of what to do and need someone to guide or help them. Luckily, there are other people who, when the "shit hits the fan" (a favorite phrase of my mother's—she has a pretty good sense of humor herself) can take charge and get things done.

Bob showed he was the latter kind of person early on. They were visiting Edith's folks, who lived in Victor, Utah. When Bob was about ten years old, he and a couple of girls who were friends of the family (I could not find anyone who remembered their names) were playing on a frozen pond. None of them had money for ice skates, but they were having a good time skidding across the pond in their boots and seeing how far they could slide. They had all been out on the pond for a while. They figured they were safe since the ice seemed thick enough. They hadn't heard it creak as they played.

Without warning, one of the girls fell through the ice.

Thinking fast, Bob flopped down on his belly and scooted over to the hole. He'd been told by his dad that if he spread his weight out, the rest of the ice was less likely to crack. He also knew with absolute certainty that if he dropped into that pond, they would both die. Bob grabbed the girl's hand and hung on. He hollered at the other girl, who stood frozen in fear staring at the scene, to go get help. His yell brought her to her senses, and she ran to find some adults.

Bob kept hanging on. It took long enough that he was certain his grip would give out before anyone could help them. He and the girl stared into each other's faces and saw the same fear. She was going to die. No one would get there in time.

After what seemed an eternity, he heard shouts and boots clomping, coming their way. He also could hear the high voices of women. The footsteps stopped advancing. They stomped back and forth at the shoreline.

"Keep hanging on, Bobby," one of the men shouted. "They're almost here with a rope."

Bob didn't recognize that voice, but he did recognize his sisters Norma and Junie as they shouted along with the men: "Hang on, Bobby!"

Not long after that, he heard an odd scraping, screeching sound. Moments later, a lariat slapped the back of his head and splashed into the water where the girl had broken through.

"Stick your free arm through that," the same voice ordered the girl.

Bob could hear more people arriving at the edge of the pond. He took a firmer grip on his friend's arm as the girl quickly slipped one arm through the loop and then grabbed ahold of Bob again. Bob moved his elbow so the rope was under his arm, too.

"Good job, kids!" several people shouted.

"Now scoot over and get on that ladder," another man ordered.

Bob had kept his eyes locked on the girl's until then, afraid that if he looked away, he'd lose his resolve. Their fear and friendship gave them strength. It would be easier to let her slip away if he wasn't looking at her wide, terrified eyes. He tightened his grip and dared to glance over his shoulder. Now he understood what the strange noise had been. The adults had shoved a fruit ladder onto the ice. They were afraid to go out on the ice themselves. The weight of the adults would be too much. Bob scooted over until his legs and hips were on the ladder.

The ladder underneath him jerked and screeched on the ice as the adults began to pull them to shore. Bob's body felt stretched as his lower half was pulled by the ladder, and his arms kept holding the girl, whose weight pulled at him from the other direction. When the girl's body hit the thick ice, he almost lost his grip. She was suddenly much heavier, but he didn't lose her. The rope tightened around her arm and neck and hurt Bob's armpit, but the ladder idea was working. They began to slide toward shore a little faster now that the girl was lying on the ice. Still, it seemed to take forever.

She tried to scramble onto her knees when her body cleared the hole in the ice. The whole shoreline behind Bob erupted into shouts admonishing her to lie still and flat. Finally, Bob's boots hit something solid, and the ladder tipped up. They had made it to the shore.

Hands grabbed them from all sides, and Bob was lifted bodily off the ladder. Someone gently pried his fingers off his friend's arm. Then the hugging and crying began. The kids were taken to the closest house, where they were wrapped in quilts and given the very rare treat of hot chocolate.

Bob's hands hurt for an hour, he'd held on so tightly. Other than sore fingers and wet clothes, he and the girl were fine. Everyone was certain his friend would have died without Bob's quick action.

THE SPUR

The Spur is a stretch of desert near what is now called Horseshoe Canyon. June's family and two other families built homesteads there. Traces of the houses and other items can still be found if you hike up the southeast side of Horseshoe Canyon and investigate the flat-top beyond. There were three houses and a work shed at the edge of the cliffs among the cedar trees.

June was never afraid of hard work, and even though building the houses and scratching a living out of that desert was difficult, he was always hunting for a better place to settle his family.

Edith loved the desert almost as much as June. She followed him all over that country, taking their growing family with them. Bob was a tiny baby when they lived at the Spur. Edith would ride with Bob lying on a pillow she placed across the pommel (that's horse lingo for the front of the saddle).

The first canyon they looked at was called Horse Thief Canyon by the locals. It's interesting that the pamphlets say it was named Barrier Canyon before it was named Horseshoe Canyon. People who lived in the area didn't call it that.

Alma, June, and the other ranch hands often corralled horses on the cliff above the canyon. It had a natural round corral with cliffsides that are straight down for more than a hundred feet in most spots. At one end was a narrow place where it was easy to put a fence across. June ran a pipe down into the spring that ran into the canyon and up to troughs at the top. They put hay in the mangers and pumped water up into the troughs to lure both wild and ranch horses into the corral.

When the canyon was made into a park and renamed Horseshoe Canyon, the park rangers left the troughs and water pipe there.

Bob and his family were tempted to settle in the canyon since it had a spring that ran all year. Large cottonwood trees and wispy willows lined its edges. They would have shade and company—the canyon is famous for its rock art—but they decided the canyon was too remote to build a homestead on, and they looked around for other places.

If you've never been to Horseshoe Canyon, it's worth the hike. We always go in on horseback, but it's worth it even on foot to see the huge, ancient rock art panels there. They are the largest in the world.

The Great Panel at Horseshoe Canyon.

WILLY'S BOTTOM

The boiler at Willy's Bottom.

June and Edith eventually decided to try making a living at Willy's Bottom. No, it wasn't Willy's butt. The term "bottom" means an area adjacent to a river that is good land for tilling and raising crops. No one remembers now where the name Willy came from, but that was what everyone called the valley.

June's friend, Andy Moore, told him he wasn't using his desert-grazing permit anymore, which encompassed the valley, and said June could use it. The valley lies on a curve of the Green River. Altogether, it is about one hundred acres of flat land nestled between the river and the cliffs. The only way down to it at that time was a steep and winding mule trail. A "mule trail" means one you'd rather use a mule to ride down than a horse. Mules are especially sure-footed.

On the maps you'll find these days, the site is called June's Bottom, perhaps because June was the last one to settle that area of the river, but June and his family always called it Willy's Bottom. June ran cattle, grew corn and other vegetables, and generally earned a meager living for his growing family. They would stay in the valley, living in the dugout during spring and summer, then spend the winters in Hanksville or Green River so the older kids could go to school.

Bob first traveled to Willy's Bottom when he was three years old. From where they lived then, it was a forty-mile ride to the town of Green River. Cowboys were not the only ones who were tough back then.

June's dad, Alma, settled there first. The river froze over that year. It was quite a lot closer to a road from the other side of the river, so they drove the cattle and horses to a break in the cliffs where they had access to the river. To get the cattle and horses over to the valley, they put leather straps on their hooves so they wouldn't slip on the ice, and they crossed the river that way. Since there was good grazing in the valley, they knew the livestock would stay there. Once the ice broke up, Alma came down the river in his canoe and put up a wall tent. Then he and June began building a dugout and a road so they could bring supplies in by wagon.

They didn't use the river water for drinking because there was too much alkali in it. Their water supply was a natural spring that ran most of the year, although sometimes in the late summer it would dry up. Three Canyons is very near Willy's Bottom and has a spring that runs all year. When the spring at Willy's Bottom dried up, June and Alma would go to Three Canyons to get water and float the barrels down the river. Every time I hear that, I think of how convenient it is these days to take only a few steps and have clean, fresh water from the tap.

The spring did not provide enough water for irrigating crops. To make a go of living there, they needed more water. Once the road was complete, Alma and June brought a boiler and pump in using a wagon and team. They set it up near the river not far from the dugout. They would jack up the Model T car they had and hook a line from the car axle to the boiler to run the pump. That way, they could irrigate the garden and cornfield.

It took two years of working on the road before they could get the car in there.

THE PET BULL

Heading for Willy's Bottom on the Green River, following the road that June
built. September 2003.

In 2001, the Bureau of Land Management (BLM) was proposing
closing vehicle access to the road June built that leads to Willy's
Bottom. They claimed no one had ever lived there. I remember
reading the court transcript. It was fascinating because it had not
even occurred to the people questioning Bob that he had *lived*
down there. And it didn't occur to Bob that they didn't know that.

The BLM attorney would ask questions like "What was the
purpose of the road?" and Bob would answer, "Well, so we could
get a wagon down in there."

It went on like that, and I don't think either party ever

understood the other's perspective. Or perhaps the BLM attorneys didn't want to *listen*.

The Marsings wanted the road to stay open to vehicles because many of the family members were no longer able to travel in on horseback or hike. The closest maintained dirt road is still fifteen miles from the dugout.

One day, Bob's niece Alona was at the grocery store and picked up a *Four-Wheel Drive* magazine for her husband and son to read. A group of four-wheel enthusiasts had been across the river checking out the sights and noticed the road that June built. They decided to try to find a way to get to the road. Eventually they did find it, and they took pictures of the dugout and old boiler. When Alona saw the article, she called my mom, and Mom went out and bought some of the magazines. At the end of the article was the email address of the photographer.

Mom contacted him, and they arranged for a group of four-wheel enthusiasts to help take Bob and others from his family who could no longer ride horseback into the dugout. A garden variety of twenty-six vehicles trailed Bob across the desert and down into Willy's Bottom.

Utah's channel four had a TV show called *At Your Leisure*. Chad Booth was the producer. One of the Jeep enthusiasts asked him if he wanted to come along on the trip to Willy's Bottom. He thought that was a great idea and took his Jeep and a cameraman and headed across the desert with the rest. The program aired in 2002.

When they were all down there exploring the valley, Bob told the following story, although the version he told when cameras weren't rolling was a little more colorful.

June was on his way out of the dugout to work on improving the watering holes they had for the horses and cattle. Doug Wells, Edith's little brother, was living with them at the time. He was about ten years old. As June left to ride up the road, Edith heard June tell Doug to go get the milk cows out of the pasture. The cow pasture lay at the lower end of Willy's Bottom.

The Wells clan (Edith's family) had brought some of their cattle over to add to June and Alma's herd. The Wells family lived in Hanksville, but Doug spent a lot of his time with Alma and June.

Bob thought it was great that he had an older boy to look up to.

Doug disappeared for quite a while, but when he came back, he didn't have the milk cows with him. Edith asked him why he hadn't brought the cows in, and he said the bull wouldn't let him. Exasperated, she told Doug to find June and tell him. The family needed the milk.

June was not happy to stop his work and berated Doug all the way back to the little valley. He growled about that bull being "pet raised," and all it would take was a can of grain for him to follow you anywhere. He said that bull was "tame as a puppy" and just had Doug and Edith buffaloed.

When they got to the dugout, June's saddle horse was done in (really tired), so he tied it up and caught one of the big plow horses. June was still cussin' and grumbling about how he had to take care of that pet-raised bull while he fashioned a halter out of some rope and put it on the plow horse. Then he climbed on bareback and went to the pasture to show Doug how things were done.

When June opened the pasture gate and rode the big horse through, he found the bull at the far end of the big field behind some willows, guarding the cows. The bull spotted him at the same time. Right then, June knew he'd made a mistake. The bull was on the fight, and June was on a horse that was too slow. He wheeled the big bay around and kicked him into a run, hoping to make tracks before the bull caught up.

Well, plow horses are not bred for speed. The horse just could not move fast enough. The bull ran up behind them and lifted the horse's butt off the ground, and they scooted along with the old plow horse running along on only his front feet. They went like that for about fifteen or twenty feet, then the bull dropped the horse back onto all four hooves, and June tried to get more speed out him. They went all the way across the big pasture with the bull scootin' that old horse along.

When June finally made it out of the pasture, he stomped into the dugout and started tossing things around, grumbling and cussing under his breath, looking for something. Edith asked what he was after, and he said, "My pistol! I'm gonna shoot that son of a bitch!"

By all accounts, Edith was a brave woman. She said, "Why, that ole pet-raised bull just has you buffaloed."

The next morning, Bob watched while the bull was laid down a bull and got back up a steer, his hormonal problem solved.

LIZARD GRAVY

Junie, Bobby, and Norma, 1932.

Life at Willy's Bottom was rough, but as Bob pointed out more than once, it wasn't that different from living in town in those days, since even in town no one had indoor plumbing or electricity. They had a lot of visitors, even as isolated as they were. Still, the closest town was fifteen miles away—and that was across country. It was forty miles by road.

Bob's nature was to see the fun in life. He thought it was a great place to live since they had lots of rocks to climb, sand to play in, and a river to wish they could swim in (they weren't allowed to actually swim in the river).

Bob's world as a small boy revolved around his dad. He was June's shadow and followed him and his grandpa Alma wherever they went, all over the valley. Unless he was teasing his sisters. Like most little boys, he figured he was a "big man" and could do what the grownups did.

Alma chewed tobacco. One day, Bob found the package where Alma had set it down. He was about four years old. I think every boy in those times tried chewing tobacco at least once. Bob was no exception. He took a chunk of it like he'd seen the men do and chewed it. He hadn't noticed that the men didn't swallow it, so he gulped it down. You can imagine how bad that burned. Bob was sick for days and never chewed tobacco again.

Kids can find something fun to do almost anywhere. There was a little island near where Alma and June had placed the boiler. Bob's sisters, Norma and Junie, would wash dishes near there. They would float the plates and other things in the little channel between the island and the bank to see which would win the "race." It was also the perfect place to make mud pies and sandcastles.

They shared the valley with rattlesnakes—lots of them. Country folks learn things that are rarely seen in books. For instance, rattlesnakes travel in pairs. If you see one, there is likely another close by.

Bob had a little dog named Toby that went everywhere he did. The dog was expert at killing rattlesnakes and never did get bitten. He'd snatch them right behind the head and shake them until they died.

When they could get away with it in the summer, Bob and his sisters would make a little dam up by the spring and play in the water there. They had to take care not to get too close to the poison oak that grew in abundance, and the stubborn plants always came back no matter how often June and Alma tore them out.

The dugout really was a dug-out. The back half of it was cut into the hillside, and the remaining walls were made of sandstone blocks. In that part of the country, sandstone breaks off in even slabs that look like they have been manufactured. It makes for a very nice wall. The stone walls help a house stay cool much better than wood and plaster. The roof was cedar poles covered with sod and clay. Today, parts of two walls are still there, as well as the springs from the mattress. The boiler is gone; someone finally hauled it off. Someone also stole the rope maker that used to stand

29

between the dugout and the chicken coop.

The family had beef and corn to eat, as well as other vegetables and canned goods. They grew a few vegetables and melons each summer. Food was scarce and not to be wasted.

During their second summer in the valley, Edith's sister, Elverna, and her family were visiting. Aunt Ernie (Norma called Elverna that when she was a toddler, and the name stuck) and Edith decided to make biscuits and gravy to feed the crowd. It was all they could think up to feed everyone who had come to visit that day on such short notice.

Aunt Ernie was making biscuits, and Edith was stirring the big frying pan full of gravy when a little lizard fell into the frying pan. It had been crawling along the cedar log above her. Edith fished the critter out and went on cooking. After all, there was no sense in wasting all that good food. The kids remember that Edith and Aunt Ernie didn't eat that evening. A few years later, Edith confessed to what happened and never did hear the end of it after that.

Junie, Bob, and Doug in front of the dugout.

SELLING "MAPS"

June was an enterprising man and was always on the lookout for ways to earn a little more money. It wasn't that hard to trade work for things, but cash money was hard to come by. Times were tough in the 1930s. He and his brother, Bill, found gold somewhere down in that remote desert. The family has an aspirin bottle with the gold dust in it. But June and Bill weren't able to make a go of it with that, and they never did disclose the location of their source to others in the family.

Prohibition was in full swing when they were living at Willy's Bottom. June could raise cattle and vegetables to feed his family, but he also needed a cash crop. June raised corn for feeding his cattle, but he didn't use it only for livestock.

June had grown up in that wild country. When raising cattle down there, it wasn't long before the cowboys knew just as well as the cows where water could be found. June would put a packsaddle on a couple of horses and load them up with corn, sugar, and equipment and head off for one of the dozens of small, remote canyons that make up what is now Canyonlands National Park.

Down in the canyon next to the water, he would set up a still and run off a batch of moonshine. He was careful to bank the small fire just so, ensuring it would not escape or get too hot. Then he would head back home. Once the moonshine was finished cooking, he would keg it up and bury the booze. Once that was done, he would draw up a map to locate it. Then he'd take down the still and move it to another watering hole.

June was a pleasant man and could make friends with almost

anyone. But in those days, when he went to town to get supplies, he'd have more than the usual crowd wanting to come for a chat. They all knew June sold "maps."

June had a lot of dreams, but very few came to fruition. The whole family loved living at Willy's Bottom, but they eventually had to move away. The cattle kept getting into the poison oak. No matter how June and Alma tried, they could not rid the valley of that pesky plant (it's still there). The milk would make them sick, especially Edith, so they packed up and moved on.

THE CAT RANCH

June's favorite occupation was ranching and breaking in horses, whether they were tame or wild. He worked for several cattlemen throughout central Utah as a cattle drover and sold horses he'd trained for extra cash. He gained a reputation for being a good man to fix up a ranch and maintain it. Ranchers would then let him and his family live on their ranch while he got it operational.

June had a friend who owned the Cat Ranch. The place was run down, and June was hired to get it up and running. As with many of the homes Bob lived in as a boy, the ranch was miles from the closest paved road (it still is). His parents had packed up their wagon with supplies, loaded the kids in, and headed for the ranch.

By the time they made it to the long road that leads to the Cat Ranch it was dark, and the temperature had gone down quite a bit. Clouds of steam came off the horse's backs as they walked up the road. They still had quite a far stretch to go. It had been snowing for a while. A couple of inches of new snow lay on the wagon road.

Bob was bored and began his favorite pastime: tormenting his sisters. The kids were all weary from riding in the wagon. Besides, it was cold.

June and Edith got tired of the children complaining and told them they could get down from the wagon and walk on ahead. When they scrambled down, Edith warned them to stay in the road where they could see their tracks.

Bob and his sisters trotted up the track for a while until they were so far ahead they couldn't hear the wagon anymore. The snow stopped falling and the clouds parted, revealing a clear sky full of stars. Norma remembered thinking how pretty it was with the new pristine snow sparkling in the moonlight—until Bob hit her with a snowball. Then the fight was on. They were all chucking snow at each other when they heard the wagon clattering up behind them with the horses at a run.

June and Edith were yelling at the top of their lungs, and the wagon was rattling along, making a real racket. The kids stepped off the road, wondering what had gotten into their parents. Norma thought maybe the horses had spooked and were running away with the wagon.

June and Edith had been driving the wagon along, following the kids' tracks and chatting about things that would need to be done to get the ranch up and going. Then they saw a chilling sight. Large cougar tracks came out of the brush, turned, and followed the kids' shoe prints up the road.

As soon as they saw that, June whipped up the team (that's horse-speak for getting them moving faster) and charged up the track, yelling at the top of his lungs and cracking his whip, hoping to scare the cat away. The cat must have been hungry because it persisted in following the kids' tracks until the wagon was in sight. Then the big cat's tracks veered off the road.

The kids only saw a flash of tawny coat move into the brush. It had been within yards of them. After that, people called the ranch "The Cat Ranch."

CHAPPY

The summer after the family left Willy's Bottom, they spent the fall living at Granite and then moved onto the Cat Ranch. A rancher who was friends with June gave him his old worn-out racehorse, Chappy, to use for pulling the wagon. Since Norma was the oldest, June told her she could have the horse to ride when he wasn't hooked to the wagon.

Bob was jealous that his sister had a horse of her own, so he adopted an orphan lamb and kept it as his own the same summer Norma got Chappy. He wouldn't even let them chop the lamb's tail off. He and the lamb went everywhere together. To make up a little for Bob's lack of a horse, June made Bob a pair of his own cowboy boots so he could be like his dad. He was his dad's shadow, after all. He wore those boots until his toes showed out of the ends.

Old Chappy's feet wouldn't hold up to hard roads with the weight of a rider, so he was a safe mount for Norma. He wouldn't go too fast out on the road and would stick around by the house. But on soft dirt, that horse was lightning fast.

June's friend Lawrence Ekker was often at the Cat Ranch and was always bragging about how fast his horses were. He said there was no chance that old gray horse could outrun his. He'd heard that Chappy was a former racehorse.

One day when Lawrence came to visit Bob, who at that time was a wiry little kid about seven years old, bet Lawrence that Chappy could outrun his horse even facing backward. Lawrence took him up on the bet.

What Lawrence didn't know was that Bob and Norma had been

practicing racing Chappy in the plowed field that was up behind the house. The old horse's feet would give out after just a little bit, but he could last until the end of the field. Old Chappy would hop up and down if he was facing the track/field, but he'd stand good when he faced the other way. Then, when Norma wheeled him around, he'd take off.

Bob wasn't the only one who liked a good horse race. The Ekkers and Marsings who were there that day lined up on the edge of the field to watch the race. So, with a teenage Norma riding bareback and facing away from the field, she took on that cowboy riding in a saddle and mounted on a much younger horse. Old Chappy left Lawrence in the dust that day, and Bob collected his winnings, being careful to do it out of Edith's sight—gambling being a sin and all. After that, Bob was hooked on horse racing.

LAMB DINNER

June said later that he thought the cougar was after their orphan mule the night the cat followed the kids in the snow. The little mule had been adopted by Chappy and followed him everywhere he went. On that first trip to the Cat Ranch, he would run along ahead of the wagon, tromping in the snow and bucking.

Ranchers know things that scientists have never cottoned on to. For some reason, cougars like the taste of mules. They'll pass by a horse and choose mule meat every time unless there's a sheep around. Mules and sheep have a stronger odor than horses, so maybe that's why.

Bob's cousin Homer lived down in that country not far from the Cat Ranch and raised sheep. One year during lambing season, Homer went out to the shed to check on the sheep. The shed had a low roof to keep the heat in better.

Nights are cold in the desert, even in midsummer, and it was early spring. Sheep are always skittish, but Homer noticed they were unusually nervous as he walked to the back of the shed to check on a ewe that was lying down. She looked like she was ready to lamb anytime.

He bent down to look her over. The small herd of sheep swept around the side of the shed and crowded next to Homer and the ewe, who had not gotten up. It was odd for them to get so close. They were range sheep and weren't very tame. Then he caught movement of a different kind out of the corner of his eye.

A cougar was in the shed, slinking along only about ten feet from him. The cat's ears were flat back, and he was moving along so low his belly was sliding on the straw. Homer and the cat stared at each other. He was thinking fast but not coming up with much in the way of options. The cat was between him and the gate. Plus, he didn't have a gun or even shoes on. It was the middle of the night, and he hadn't bothered putting boots on to check for new lambs.

Homer had a moment to consider the thought that maybe he could toss one of the sheep at the cat if it came closer. Luckily, he had not shut the outer door all the way. The cat seemed to weigh his options too. Then it whirled around and darted away. It jumped the gate at the end of the shed and scooted out the door. Bob said he was tempted to ask Homer if he had to put on new shorts when he got back to the house, but he never did ask.

***

They often had visitors while they were living at the Cat Ranch. It was one of the few places in the area with an actual house, not just a wall tent. The government sent out surveyors to map the Henry Mountains, and they would stay at the ranch. They had an archeologist named Alice visit for a while, and one surveyor, Alice's brother-in-law Lee Hunt, would come out and stay all summer.

It's not hard to guess how the ranch came by its name. It's quite rare to lay eyes on a cougar, but tracks are a common sight. The ranch is still there. At the entrance to the road leading up to the ranch, petrified trees lay strewn about. During the uranium boom of the 1950s, the miners knew if they followed the trees into the ground they would find the right kind of ore. So they pulled the trees out when they mined.

GOIN' TO POT

Does your family have favorite phrases? Mine does. One of those is "things go to pot." To translate, that means things sometimes go wrong for no apparent reason. I could write another whole book about things like that. Anyway, this story was memorable enough that Bob recalled it even though he was only about four.

June and his brother Lon were driving June's Model T truck across Antelope Flats, which is part of the Beryl desert, on their way to Willy's Bottom. The truck was loaded down with kids, hay, and chicken pens.

Norma was squished in the middle with Bob on her lap. As the truck rattled along the desert track, she thought she smelled smoke and asked her dad what it was. June looked over at her, and his eyes went wide.

June slammed on the brakes. He and Lon started tossing kids, chicken pens, hay, and everything else within reach out onto the sand and cheatgrass so they could get to the fire. It turned out the battery behind the seat had shorted out and started the hay on fire.

They got the fire out soon enough and didn't lose much hay, but the kids had to sit out in that desert for several hours with only the water jug they kept for the truck radiator. They put hay bales over the chicken pens so the birds wouldn't cook in their cages in the heat, but all the kids had as a reprieve from the sun was a big rock that offered a small patch of shade.

Eventually, June and Lon came back with another vehicle and a battery, and they made it to Willy's Bottom.

Speaking of that old Model T, have you ever read the book *The*

Grapes of Wrath, or watched the movie? It's an excellent story about hardship and attitude. June's family lived a life very similar to that one year. There wasn't enough work for June to make a living in the desert, and the grass had all dried up due to the drought that an entire third of the United States was trapped in.

June heard of some land available in Sand Point, Idaho, so he loaded the truck with his kids, a few meager supplies, and stuck their mattress on top just like in the movie. When they arrived in Sand Point, they found the land was no good. There wasn't work back in Utah, so June took them north and west.

Bob spent most of the year he was ten wandering the west with his family while they took any work they could find. Most of it was following the crops as they ripened. They picked apples in Yakima, Washington, and Hood River, Oregon. Then they headed south, picking hops, tomatoes, and beans in California. Eventually, they came to the coast where Bob saw the ocean for the first time on Thanksgiving Day.

When the harvest was over, June decided to head back to his sister's place in Beryl, Utah. The family arrived on the day Pearl Harbor was bombed.

Bob had left his horse, named Flax, with Doug to care for while they went on their "fruit tramp" trip. That's what Bob's family called themselves that year. Doug was working as a ranch hand and was using Flax as a pack horse.

Doug was crossing the Dirty Devil River when Flax tripped and went down on his knees. When he did, the pack bags filled with water and the pack was too heavy for Flax to stand back up. The horse ended up drowning. So, when Bob arrived back in Utah, he once again didn't have a horse of his own. It was not a good year for Bob or anyone else in the family.

These days, parents watch their kids like eagles. Most parents require a text or a phone call the minute the kid goes anywhere, and even teenage children are rarely left on their own. Times have changed. When Bob was twelve, he spent the entire summer alone on the mountain near Navajo Lake, Utah, caring for a herd of buck sheep owned by his dad's friend, Bob Fenton.

When he was fourteen, Bob got a job with Bob Fenton again

to trail a herd of beef cattle from Cedar City, Utah, to Sand Springs, Nevada. There were two other boys with him, but Bob was in charge because he could drive and get supplies in Caliente, Nevada, when they needed them. The restaurant with the punched tin ceiling and the train station are still there.

I wonder what kids these days would think of living like that. There was no internet, phones, TV, or even electricity. Only your imagination and grit.

Although living was rough, Bob always saw a chance to have some fun. He could invent his own entertainment. One of his favorite things was to hide a bag of potatoes near the church house. He and a couple of other teenagers would sneak out between services and push the potatoes into the exhaust pipes of a few cars and trucks.

Then they'd dawdle after church instead of heading home just to hear the potatoes explode like a shotgun blast. The best part, in Bob's opinion, was hearing those good church-going people cuss.

ROSALEE AND LOIS

People are sometimes granted a glimpse of what the future will bring. Edith was a person with that gift—or curse, depending on your perspective. It makes me wonder how time really works. It must not be entirely linear, because sometimes things will be seen in a vivid dream, or a flash of insight, that hasn't happened yet.

When Rosalee was born, Edith was struck with a premonition that she wouldn't live very long. She was sure of it. The memory bothered her, but as Rosalee grew, she set her worry aside and enjoyed her little girl.

Rosalee was ahead of things from the start. She walked at nine months, and when she was eleven months old could repeat anything anyone told her. She was small and pretty with blonde hair and big, blue eyes. She followed her sisters Norma and Junie around like a happy little puppy and seemed to be growing up just fine.

When she was six years old, Edith gave Rosalee a small purse with a few coins in it for Christmas. Rosalee was very excited to get the chance to spend real coins the next time they were in town. On New Year's Day, June went outside to kill a beef, and Edith told the kids to come inside.

She said, "You don't want to see that poor animal killed."

Rosalee piped up and said, "Oh, that's not bad. It is not bad to die."

That night, Rosalee woke up crying. She had a big, blue lump behind her ear and dark spots on her neck and chest. Edith took her into town to see the doctor, and he said she would need her tonsils out.

Edith sent for June. While they waited, Rosalee asked if she could go to the drug store to spend her money. Edith was too worried about her little girl to go to the store and said they should wait until after the doctor took care of her.

Rosalee said, "I won't ever get to spend my money."

She died on January third, two days later. They called it Purpla (an infection of the Mastoid joint behind the ear), which is not a term used these days.

We are so lucky in this modern era to be spared the fear of disease that people lived with daily. Human beings still battle such things, but not in the numbers we used to.

***

When Edith was pregnant with Rosalee, she had a vivid dream. In the dream, a little girl with wispy blonde hair and bright blue eyes walked up to her carrying a baby and said, "Will this baby do?" When she grew to be a toddler, Edith realized the girl holding the baby in her dream was Rosalee.

Lois Marsing was born one year and two months after Rosalee died. She was a mirror image of Rosalee and was advanced for her age like her sister had been. When she was two, she could keep up with the older kids when they joked around talking in Pig Latin.

Bob was fascinated with his little sister. He loved to carry her around and make her laugh at the funny faces he made. Although when she got a little older, he didn't waste any time teasing her as much as he did his big sisters.

On Christmas Day, when Lois was six, Edith bought her a pair of brown and white shoes. That night, Edith woke up from a nightmare and sat bolt upright. June asked her what was wrong. She said, "I've bought her a pair of shoes just like Rosalee had on when she died."

June comforted her and said not to worry, it was just a dream.

The next day, the families from Hanksville went up into the Henry Mountains to gather pine nuts. Large piles can often be found in pack rat nests. They brought them back and washed them, then built a fire to roast them over. It was a normal thing they had done every winter since anyone could remember.

Lois got sick two days later. In fact, several people in town were sick at the same time. It was spinal meningitis. Lois died in January of 1938. She only lived a year longer than her sister had.

If you visit the graveyard in Hanksville, you'll notice a disturbing similarity in many of the dates of death in 1938, especially the children.

When I read things like that, I'm struck by how lucky I am to have lived my life now, in this time and place. I like horses, and I don't mind dirt under my fingernails or working hard, but I enjoy my creature comforts, too. I like fresh, clean water from the tap at any temperature I want, and food right there in the fridge. Or, if what I want isn't there, it's just a quick trip to the store. It's easy to feel nostalgic about those times, and countless movies and books have been written painting the rugged life people lived then as romantic and adventurous. But the reality was that life was a struggle. You literally had to scrape a living from the earth and hope disease or danger didn't take your children away before they had a chance to grow up.

No, they weren't really the "good old days." As much as we like to romanticize those days as a simple life with less stress, it isn't really true. We like to complain today about the sad state of things, but the lives we live daily are far easier than the lives most people led in the good old days.

LEGACY

When June passed away, he didn't leave his family with anything in the form of monetary value. What he gave his family was far more valuable. His children were all hardworking, with a readiness to jump in and help others with a smile on their faces. They were honest, decent people who were true to their family and friends. And most of all, through June's example, he gave his son a gift more precious than a vault full of treasure: to view every day with joy and to spread that love of living to those around you.

LIFE AT RED CLIFF RANCH

The earliest known photograph of the Red Cliff Ranch.

GRANDPA MARSING

Annabelle, Alma, family, and friends in front of the main house at the ranch.

I'm not sure who Bob learned his storytelling talent from, but I think he got his start from his Grandpa Marsing, and then it was enhanced by his dad. At the turn of the twentieth century, Alma Marsing built a ranch from scratch until it encompassed more than a section of land (a section is 640 acres). By the time Alma was done building his ranch, he had a main house and fourteen out-buildings (bunkhouses, blacksmith shop, school/bunkhouse, the main house, guest houses, stables, coops, corncrib, pig and cow pens, etc.). He'd built miles of road and irrigation ditches using a horse-drawn scraper, and he managed several more sections of land for grazing and raising hay in partnership with other people.

That was before the dry years in the late twenties and thirties. At the turn of the century, there was more rainfall. The annual rainfall then was such that the grass would grow knee-high and willow trees lined the river instead of tamarisk. June told Bob that when he was a boy, you could cross the Price River almost anywhere. The sand hadn't fallen away to make cliffs and steep banks yet.

Alma and Annabelle had six children. June was the third. His older brothers were Harv and Lon. His younger siblings were Nick, Bill, Mel, Della, and Rose. They moved onto the Red Cliff Ranch in 1908. June was eight years old. Few men have the kind of character it takes to decide to start up a big ranch and make it successful. Alma did. The ranch he built from nothing out in a remote desert prospered for two decades and grew until they had seven hundred head of cattle and two hundred head of horses.

GRIT

Everyone loved living at the ranch, but it was not an easy life. Kids had to be responsible and grew up fast. It wasn't only the men and boys who were tough. June had two little sisters. The summer Rose was six and Della was eight, they would ride their horses out to the hayfield and fill a sack with green alfalfa for the chickens to eat. They were on their way back when Rose's horse ran away with her. She was within about three hundred yards of the house when the strap on one of the tin spurs she was using to stay on with snapped in two. She landed on the road and broke her right thighbone.

June was the only one home that morning. Everyone else was out in the fields tending to the livestock. He caught the horse and backtracked it until he found Rose. He scooped her up and took her to the house. Della rubbed Mentholatum on her leg while June hitched up the team. Then they started out.

Every time they hit a rut or a rock in the road, Rose didn't cry— she would cuss and scream. June didn't know she knew some of those words. It scared him so bad he turned the wagon around and went back to the house. He found a long board and bound her leg up so it was straight, then saddled up his horse and went to find the doctor. He made the twenty-five miles to the doctor's place in only two and a half hours! But it was the next day before the doctor could get out to the ranch. They took Rose to the hospital, and her leg was in bad enough shape that she stayed for a month.

THE SCHOOLHOUSE

The schoolhouse at the Red Cliff Ranch.

Alma and his sons worked the ranch along with some hired hands. They needed around fifteen men to keep the ranch going. There were guest houses for those with families, and the hired hands slept in the bunkhouse. It was isolated enough that Alma hired a schoolteacher and built her a house. Her name was Doll Johnson, and all the boys had a crush on her. The bunkhouse, which had originally been the first home there, served as the schoolhouse during the day.

The boys slept with the other single men in that bunkhouse.

This was a time before indoor plumbing. You had to go to the outhouse to go to the bathroom. None of the men kept chamber pots under the bed; that was a city thing. Desert air doesn't hold the heat in, and even in midsummer the nights are cold, and in winter it's downright frigid. The boys didn't want to go all the way out to the outhouse when it was below freezing. Next to June's cot was a knot in the cedar log. June worked at the knot until it came out of the log, which made a hole to the outside. He and his brothers started using the hole instead of going to the outhouse. They would plug the hole with a rag to keep the wind out.

Alma found out what they were doing and, disgusted with such behavior, told them they better stop. He only gave warnings once. About a week later, Alma found out the boys had ignored him. He didn't say anything; he just plugged the hole from the outside in such a way that it would seem to the boys to still be open.

It was June who found out the hole was plugged. They went to the outhouse after that.

THE SHEPHERD

There were more people living in that part of central Utah than there are now, but it was still desolate, and a long way from any assistance such as policemen. A rancher had to dole out his own brand of justice. If he got the reputation of waiting for the police or marshal to help him out, he'd soon have no cattle or horses left. Alma was as tough as they come, and he owned or leased a vast stretch of desert for grazing and bottomland for raising crops. His ranch prospered because of his will and his character.

One day Alma and June were riding to Green River with a couple of pack horses. They needed supplies for the ranch. June was in his late teens. When they came to where the Old Ivy Place is now, they found a large herd of sheep grazing in the valley by the small stream called Icelander Wash that flows past the Ivy Place.

Cattlemen, in general, don't like sheep. The reason is practical. Sheep are smaller and can cut the grass so short the cattle won't have anything to eat. Horses are even worse than sheep for cutting grass too short. But horses, being picky eaters, leave clumps of grass behind that the cattle can graze on. Sheep will eat everything in a pasture down to nothing in no time.

Alma rode up to the man and told him in no uncertain terms that when they got back from Green River, those sheep better not be on his land. He pointed out to the man where the edge of his property was, and they rode away.

Two days later, they were on their way back, and that herd of sheep was still grazing the same valley. They were strung along the stretch of high ground where the narrow-gauge railroad tracks had been. The metal rails had been removed from the track, but the hand-hewn wooden ties were still there.

As June relayed the story to Bob, Alma didn't say a word, he just took out his gun. June took the gun away from him, so Alma shook out a loop on his lariat, roped the shepherd under the armpits, and dragged him down the railroad tracks for about a quarter mile. When they stopped it took a minute or two, but the man was able to take the lariat off. Alma still didn't say anything. June told Bob the man's face was hardly recognizable. Alma and June gathered up their pack string and headed back to the ranch.

When June rode over with his brother to check things out the next day, the shepherd and his sheep were nowhere in sight.

CHARLIE GRIMES' CABIN

When we ride into the Old Ranch these days, we go down Stove Gulch and cross the Price River at the mouth of the gulch. Charlie Grimes' old cabin is right across the river.

Alma made a deal with Charlie Grimes, as he had with a few others, to settle on a section of land and build a cabin. Alma would then use the land for his ranch. In that way, Alma could use more land for grazing and crops than the section he owned in the official records. Alma didn't have any trouble with Charlie himself. Charlie was rarely at his cabin because he and his friends were a little loose in their interpretation of the law.

That part of Utah was a sort of thoroughfare for outlaws. It was easy for a gang to lose themselves among the desolate, barren area south of the ranch in what is now called Canyonlands. No posse in their right minds would pursue men into those canyons. There were far too many likely places for an ambush. Besides, although there were many canyons to hide in, water was scarce. It was easier for law enforcement to stake out the places where water could be found or wait where the river or stream comes out of a canyon.

Alma's ranch lay in the middle of that "outlaw highway." Because of his reputation, he never did have trouble with thieves stealing his livestock or equipment, at least not permanently.

There were many times when horses would disappear from Alma's fields, and some worn-out horses they had never seen would be in their place. A month or so later, or sometimes even half a year later, Alma's horses would show up in the field, and the strange horses would be gone. Sometimes, Alma's horses would be thin and tuckered out when they came back. But most often, the outlaws would leave the horses with a fresh set of shoes on, and they would be fit and sleek.

They did lose a few cattle to rustlers, as nearly all cattlemen do even today, but most people knew not to bother with Alma's property. They knew the man was too tough to cross.

Bob at Annabelle's grave.

THE GRAVESTONE

The year June turned eighteen, his mother, Annabelle, took sick. Her heart was failing, but she thought it was the flu. She didn't want them to take her to a doctor because she was afraid she would get others sick. She and Alma both knew she wasn't going to make it; she had been sick for months. They had loved each other very much from the start. They were a study in opposites. She had dark hair and eyes and carried a solemn and serious air about her. Alma was a sandy-haired Swede with pale-blue eyes who liked a good joke.

Alma had a lot of drive and try, and he taught his kids to be the same way. He was continually working to improve the ranch until Annabelle died. That took the wind out of his sails. The family said that when she died, they buried Alma, too. All that was left was a ghost of the man he had been.

Perhaps the most beautiful vista the Old Ranch has to offer is the spot where Annabelle's grave is.

Some hikers found her grave one time and made it part of an article they wrote about their desert trip. They guessed it was the grave of some poor shepherd. Annabelle's name is scratched onto the sandstone rock Alma placed at the head of her grave, but the hikers didn't seem to have noticed that. One of the Marsings ran across the article and brought it to Bob's attention.

Bob's family decided to make a gravestone and place it at the grave. It would be a family reunion of sorts. Once again, a long string of vehicles and trailers followed Bob across the desert to Stove Gulch. There were several cousins along that time. Only six of us had horses. The others decided to bring along a rubber raft and float across the river, then walk in. I didn't envy those who were on foot; it's a *very* long walk.

Bob fashioned a wooden box with handles on the sides to carry the stone in. When we made it to the fence that is the beginning of the ride into the Gulch, people were surprised—they assumed one of the horses would be packing in the stone.

Bob's nephew Scott Burton and Danny (a friend) helping carry the new gravestone to Annabelle's grave. 1994.

Bob explained before we arrived that there is a narrow spot that won't fit a horse with a pack on, and he also didn't trust a horse to get the stone there in one piece. He said, not for the first time, that was why he asked for lots of people to come. So they could take turns carrying the stone.

When we arrived at Stove Gulch, Bob was outnumbered in the vote on whether they would use a horse or not. We looked at the horses assembled, and the only one that wasn't wild-eyed from being in a new place was Clyde. The gelding (neutered horse) was only four years old, but he was calmer and steadier than any of the others.

We looked at the stone, at the box it was in, and at the horse, trying to figure out how to rig up a way for the horse to carry it. The stone was too heavy to sling over one side, and we didn't have a pack bag or a suitable counterweight.

There are more stories about Clyde later in this book. In fact, the horse has his own chapter. Since this part of the book is about the gravestone, you'll learn a little about Clyde before you get to read the rest of his story. He was half draft horse, so he was a big boy. He was good-natured and would let almost anyone ride him as long as they didn't jerk him around.

One of Bob's cousins volunteered to get on and hold the box with the gravestone in his lap, with part of the box resting on the saddle horn. He settled in the saddle, and Bob and his great-nephew Anthony hoisted that box onto his lap. They strapped it on with the saddle strings and started out.

Bob and I exchanged a look. We were sure this wasn't going to work out. I figured if it did, I was going to have a long way to walk. Cowboy boots are not designed for long walks.

Things went okay for a few hundred yards until they came to a spot where the trail went downhill. When the gravestone shifted, the sand underneath it squeaked. Clyde thought that was a little weird, so he sidled sideways. The box squeaked some more. Bob's cousin had his arms full of box and gravestone and couldn't steer the horse very well. Bob and I jogged over toward them in an attempt to get ahold of Clyde's bridle, but we were a second too late.

Clyde decided he was going to get rid of that squeaky box and the stranger riding him. He humped up and hopped down that hill. The rider stuck with it, so Clyde decided to start really bucking. In no time, the gravestone went one way, the rider another, and the box ended up hanging off Clyde's side by a couple of saddle strings. He snorted at the thing hanging there a little, but since it didn't squeak anymore, he stopped and waited for us to rescue him.

No one was hurt, not even the gravestone. They landed on soft sand.

After that, five of the men took turns hauling the heavy gravestone and box the fifteen miles to the grave.

A few years later, my cousin Russell overheard us talking about the ranch. Bob commented that the only way to get in there besides on horseback was to float down the river, walk, or fly in. Russell flew Apache helicopters for the National Guard. It turns out that stretch of the Price River is often used as a landmark when the pilots practice maneuvers. Russell asked Bob a couple of pointed questions about the location as we looked at pictures of our recent trip. We didn't think any more about it until he sent Bob this photo.

Russ's Apache helicopter in front of the Schoolhouse.

ONE LAST SHOT

Edith and June.

June married Edith in Victor at eight a.m. on a beautiful Saturday morning. Edith and June said it was the only time they knew of when everybody in town got somewhere on time. They had a very nice wedding and appreciated all the thoughtfulness of the people in town and their families.

June took his new bride out to the Red Cliff Ranch to try to make a go of it. But the river had other ideas. In the fall, they had fields full of melons and corn, and several acres of alfalfa ready to harvest. Then the floods came. The river took out acres and acres of crops. The family climbed onto the roof of the house but then had to climb the hillside behind it to stay out of the water. That was the end of the Red Cliff Ranch. The buildings survived the flood, but no one has ever lived there since.

TEMPLE JUNCTION

Temple Junction when it was a "going concern."

When Bob was just past twenty and had been released from his service in the Korean War, the uranium boom began. Miners were flooding into central and southern Utah, and June had an idea. He was a smart man, after all. In any mining boom, the ones who make money are most often the merchants, not the miners. June built Temple Junction in the early fifties at the crossroads where Highway 24 met the road to Temple Mountain, which is now the road to Goblin Valley.

Temple Junction began as a spot where miners could fill up their gas tanks and stock up on beer. Eventually, there were motel rooms and a restaurant, too.

June pumping gas for a customer.

WELL DIGGIN'

Temple Junction was a going concern for several years and would have been quite profitable, except that everything had to be trucked in, even drinking water. To try to keep costs down, June ordered a well dug between the highway and the Temple Junction bar, near where Edith had planted three trees.

June set Bob, Bruce (Bob's brother-in-law), and Merril (Bob's nephew) working on it. They dug for a few days, off and on, until they reached the hardpan. Once they were down that deep (about twelve feet), it was solid rock, and they didn't have the kind of tools they needed to get through that hard layer. The three young men stood around, staring into the hole and contemplating their options.

Eventually, Bob had an idea. They sold dynamite to the miners for their uranium mines at the Junction, and he knew where it was stored. Merril and Bruce thought that was a great idea. Bob rustled up about three sticks. They tied them together and lowered them into the hole. It seemed like too little dynamite for the job, so they put another three sticks in the hole for good measure. They looked down at the dynamite for a few minutes, trying to come up with the courage to set the cord on fire. After conferring for a while, the three of them decided maybe they should stack some pallets and heavy rocks over the hole to keep the blast contained. After all, the "well" was very near both the highway and the Junction bar and café.

The sign Mom put on the tree Edith planted.

As an afterthought, they figured they should maybe stop traffic on the highway before they lit it off. They stationed a couple of "volunteers" (Bob made his sisters do it) to stop traffic on the road. Then Bob drew the short straw and had the job of lighting the cord. All three of them ran behind the Junction, put their backs to the wall, and plugged their ears.

The blast left them deaf for a quarter of an hour. It not only blew the pallet off but the main portion of its pieces, as well as the boulders they'd placed on top of it, landed across the highway—about two hundred feet. Everyone poured out of the Junction to see what the noise was about. The entire area around the buildings, including the roof, was strewn with bits of wood, tools, and rocks.

Bob didn't hear most of the words coming out of June's mouth when his dad found him since he was mostly deaf at that moment, but he got the gist.

They did find water, but every well they dug was bad water that could only be used in the garden or things like that. They had to continue trucking in drinking and wash water.

Speaking of water, one of Edith's trees is still alive. It's at the corner where the Goblin Valley road meets the highway. If you're visiting Goblin Valley or are heading for Hanksville, stop by and give the tree a drink.

WATCH YER MOUTH

Edith's brother Bill and June playing outlaw and sheriff.

Bruce and Bob spent one morning plinking at cans with June's pistol when they were supposed to be digging that well. When they were done, Bruce discovered he only had three bullets left to put in June's gun. Like most of the cowboys who carried guns in those days, June was in the practice of leaving the chamber empty that the gun was on. Bruce left that one and the two after it empty. He intended to load it and pay June back for the ammo they used once he could make it to Hanksville and back. He set the gun on the shelf under the bar where it belonged and went on about his business.

Edith was often enlisted to help tend bar when they were short-handed, even though she did not agree with drinking or the miners' foul language. She was quite busy tending to the miners, taking lunch orders and doling out drinks that day. It was hot—this was before air conditioning, and the fans in the room barely moved the air—so her temper was rather short.

A miner plopped down onto a barstool and slapped his dusty hat down where Edith had just wiped it clean. He began to loudly complain about life in general and mining in particular. Every other word was a curse, and Edith could not hold back from mentioning that he should clean up his speech.

Most of the men tolerated Edith's admonitions, even if they didn't agree with her views about drink and church. In general, they were respectful around her. But this surly miner only got louder, and he continued to cuss with Edith as his target when June came in the door. June walked over behind the bar and stood beside his wife. He told the man in a quiet tone that nevertheless carried through the room, "Watch yer mouth, stranger. You don't speak to a woman that way."

The miner glared at them both, and spouted, "I'll *blanking* say what I *blanking* want to. You and your *blank* can't *blanking* order me around!"

Once again, I must remind you about the social climate at the time. Even if June could find a policeman to help him out, it would be hours before he returned. A businessman in that country at that time could not be considered an easy target, or he would soon have no supplies and no business. No one bothered June's property because they knew the man would pursue justice and not back down.

June placed a hand on Edith's shoulder and said, "Stranger, this is my wife. I expect an apology for her, and for you to take your hat and leave."

The man stood up, pushing the barstool aside. He was clearly taller than June, and about twice as wide. "Hell no, I'll not apologize to that *blank*" Even the other miners were surprised at the word he used just then.

June took his pistol out from under the bar and pointed it at the man. "You'll get no more warnings, stranger. I own this establishment, and you will treat my wife with respect when you are in it." He cocked the gun.

The miner didn't believe June. Perhaps he thought his sheer size could intimidate. The muscles bulging under his dirty t-shirt meant he clearly spent hours with pick and shovel in hard country. The miner was not known to the others in the bar that day. But they got all sorts with the uranium boom in full swing.

June was lanky and deceptively strong, but only of average height. In the miner's eyes, June was no match for him.

It was certain June knew as much about hard living as the miner did. And he'd grown up in a place and an era when you didn't wait on the law.

Also, guns were a tool, not something used for sport. Those who knew June knew this was not an idle threat he was making. Conversation in the room toned down to a low murmur.

The miner looked June up and down and came to the wrong conclusion. He went red in the face and spouted yet another string of profanities.

June pulled the trigger. Even with the man growling at June, everyone heard the click as the hammer came down on an empty chamber.

The first click was not a surprise to those there that day. The locals followed the same rules about guns, and if they had been asked, they would have said they were fairly certain the first chamber would be empty.

The idiot miner spouted off even louder, and more profane words came out of his mouth. This time, his words were aimed at June.

June thumbed the hammer back and fired again.

Click.

Complete silence fell in the bar. Edith reached up and clung to June's shooting arm, which was held steady as he thumbed a third round into place.

The thing was, June was facing the room. Everyone had seen

the surprise on June's face when the gun didn't go off. There was no bullet in that second chamber. June didn't know Bruce had used them up.

The miner's face went white under the grime. He snatched up his hat and hurried out of the bar without speaking another word.

Bruce had accidentally saved the miner's life and June some serious jail time. They never saw that particular man again. Word got around lightning fast. For the rest of the time the Junction was in business, everyone was careful to mind their tongues when Edith was tending bar.

THE VISITOR

I took a biographical writing class at Weber State College (it wasn't a university then) when I was twenty. Our assignment was to interview someone and compose an autobiographical story from it as though the person was speaking. This story is about an incident in Bob's life as related to me by him.

***

I threw the rusty old shovel back in the bed of Bruce's red '59 Ford and climbed in, cussin' sand and bad roads in general. When I got back in the truck, we started out again. I glanced over at my brother-in-law Bruce in the driver's seat. He was concentrating on missing sandbanks and potholes. He is smaller than me at five-foot-six and looked like one of those desert gophers with a thin freckled face, short red hair, and clothes covered with desert sand. People always ended up looking the same after they'd been out there very long. Everyone had a dusty look.

The road began to wander along the Muddy River, which looked like an ugly brown snake sliding along the desert floor. Whoever had named it sure knew what they were talking about. Most folks said there was more sand in the Muddy than water. We were in the San Rafael Swell country, an awesome witness to the forces of nature that ages ago heaved the Earth's crust up through the sand and left breathtaking vistas. The tilted cliffs and ledges were in every color and revealed hidden gifts that, until the uranium boom, had only been treasures for the soul.

As the pickup bumped and rattled along the worn road, I began to wonder if anyone had been this way since they abandoned the mines. We were headed for the "Hidden Splendor" where one of the Delta mines had been. During the Uranium boom the owner, Vernon Pick, had taken one million dollars out of his mines, and my dad's Temple Junction station had been at the crossroads leading to the digs. We had once sold more booze there than any other place in central and southern Utah. Man found something dear to his heart among the blood-red cliffs and Shinarump formations that dotted this country: riches in the form of minerals.

It was 1960, and the uranium boom was over, but there were still companies looking for more, and we had been commissioned by MGM Partnership to get low-grade ore out of the dumps and around the pillars in the mines where it usually concentrated. They mixed low-grade with high-grade ore to get a better rate of recovery in processing. I always thought it was strange how uranium was often hidden in these lonely canyons that were deceptively deep. You could be bumping along in the open sand and then minutes later look around and see vermillion cliffs towering on either side. Driving between those cliffs always made me a little nervous; you never knew for sure if the river was safe. The Muddy could be running slow and sad one minute and in the next turn into a raging torrent that defied any limits man might imagine for it. A wall of mud, brush, and debris could come crashing down the canyon in a flash flood swollen by rains farther upstream.

It had been noon when we left Temple Junction, but we hadn't figured on the road being so bad. I hoped we would have enough time to find firewood and get our beds ready before dark. We knew those old cabins my dad had built would need some work; they'd been abandoned for nearly eight years. Finally, we clattered around the last curve in the road and could see the row of low tar-paper covered plank cabins that had once housed about one hundred men. They looked like lost army barracks, out of place in this mainly treeless country. We climbed out of the truck and stretched to get rid of the kinks in our legs.

"I'll go hunt up some firewood," Bruce stated, yawning and

71

throwing a sideways glance at the sun.

"There's probably some over by the river," I said, just for an answer; he knew where it was. He nodded and walked around behind the buildings where the river ran alongside the cliff.

I headed for the most likely looking cabin and peered through the door-less opening. It was a small, dusty room with an old woodburning stove at one side half-covered with a pack rat's nest. The nests decorated each corner, and I hoped there wouldn't be any rats in residence when we started tearing them down. My boots echoed on the plank floor as I walked over to the next room. The place looked eerie in the afternoon sun with the lines of sunlight streaking across the boards. This room had a couple of rusty cots on each side with its own complement of rat nests. An old door was leaning against one wall.

I wandered around through the rest of the cabins, picking up girlie magazines scattered here and there. I stacked them in the room with the cots. As I stepped to the last doorway, a chilly October breeze drifted down the canyon. I turned up the collar on my worn Levi jacket and gazed across at the sheer wall of rock towering just on the other side of the road. This was home; anyplace on this desert was home for me. My dad hauled us kids and Mom all over this area, mining, bootlegging whiskey, or herding cattle. Dad was a hardworking dreamer, but he'd had a wife and little kids when the country hit hard times. During the Depression, everyone had to scrape along, and Dad came back to the places he knew, where he could take care of us. He is a part of the desert and knew more about it than almost any man alive now. I was just beginning to realize, at thirty, how much I had missed by not paying attention when he'd talk about this wild region.

"I'll have to ask him about it some more when I get the chance," I told myself. Speaking seemed an intrusion on the silence surrounding me.

I stood looking at the cliff, enjoying the patterns of red in the rock with so many different shades that in the evening sun were tinted more deep and rich. The soft, inviting colors made the desert seem less harsh.

Slowly, that familiar unsettling feeling began to send a chill up my spine that spread to every part of me. A sense of being watched, of intruding on some ancient realm, always crept over me when the desert was still. There was more here than rugged ledges and sagebrush. These canyons are ages old, carved out of the sandstone over eons. White men were newcomers. Other people had walked these draws and riverbeds and probably stared at that same cliff. They had left only their houses and pottery, which blended with the country, unlike the mines and dumps that now scarred the land. Now we had come to dig some more. What did they think of us? Were they the "watchers" I felt, as had many other people, when I took the time to pause and absorb the beauty that is there?

The crunch of boots on gravel made me jump. Bruce was trudging around the cabin with an armload of driftwood. We spent the evening hauling in the grub and bedrolls and sweeping out rat nests. Then we took some time to hang girlie pictures on the walls.

We gabbed about mining and women while eating our potatoes and beans, then decided it was time to turn in for the night.

"Which cot you want?" Bruce asked. There was a casual, easy way between us. Since we were going to have to live here for a couple of years, I was glad it would be with someone like Bruce. Besides, my sister Junie would arrive in a few days to cook for us.

"You mean I get to pick? Sure are gullible, aren't ya!" I grinned, throwing my bedroll on the cot I chose before he could change his mind.

"Whatta you mean?" he asked, looking at me suspiciously.

"I don't want that one." I nodded at the cot across the little room. "Look at that." I pointed to a big hole in the tin roof where an old stovepipe had been. It was directly over the other bed.

"Well," Bruce sighed, giving up any protest. "If I'm sleeping there, you gotta help me put something over that hole. It looks to me like it'll rain before morning."

So we scrambled up onto the roof and looked things over. We decided to use an almost full-size piece of sheetrock that was lying near the cabins. After dragging it up there, we put six or seven rocks, as heavy as we could lift, on the sheetrock to hold it in place.

With that done, we stoked the fire in the stove and lay down to read our cowboy novels. It wasn't long before Bruce woke me by

73

turning off the gas lantern, which sputtered and flickered then finally gave up.

"Hey, what if I was reading?" I pretended offense.

"Bull, your eyes were shut," was the answer.

"I was just restin' my eyelids," I said, prodding him on.

"Huh, sure," was the sarcastic reply, then nothing. He must have been too tired to take the bait. I gave it up and noticed we were swallowed in the complete darkness of a moonless desert night.

A while later, when I had drifted off to sleep again, I heard some boards creaking, then silence. After a few moments, it came again, but I couldn't really figure out where the sound was coming from.

"Aw, cut it out, Bruce!" I mumbled, figuring he was pushing on the wall next to his bed.

"Cut it out yourself, I know that's you," came his curt reply.

I started to say some smart remark back when it became obvious that the sound was coming from the farther end of the line of cabins. The walls in the place didn't go all the way to the roof, and the room had no ceiling, just rafters running lengthways. There was a sudden distinct sound of boards taking weight. Something big was on the roof, and it was getting closer.

Tension pervaded the room; my stomach did a flip-flop, and my mouth was dry. Now it was over the next room. There was a slight pause in the sound about where the stove was. Then it slowly creaked toward us, over our roof. I could see the rafters give a little over my head. A little puff of dust floated down, and I blinked. It went on across the roof and stopped over Bruce's bed. A black, eerie silence surrounded us, worse than the sound of the creaking boards before.

With a loud scrape and clatter, the entire piece of sheetrock was slid clear of the hole, and Bruce was looking at the myriad stars in the now cloudless sky.

"Son of a bitch!" Bruce leaped clear of his cot. I could see his wild eyes in the starlight that flooded the room.

"What the hell was that!" I shouted, jumping to my feet and grabbing my hat and rifle.

We both ran for the door. The hair stood up on the back of my neck, and I gave a mighty leap out of the cabin, sure that something would land on me from the roof.

"What do you think it was?" I asked, trying to look composed.

"How would I know?" he answered, looking wildly about.

"Well, did ya see anything through the hole?" I asked.

"No, just stars." I heard him swallow hard and take a deep breath.

We stared at the roof, knowing the hole was on the other side, but neither of us dared say we were too chicken to go around and check it out. So we stood there, getting cold. Then curiosity overcame fear, and we crept around the end of the cabin. No sign of anything; nothing on the roof. The piece of sheetrock, with the rocks still on top, was hanging a little off the side.

"Think it was a cat?" Bruce inquired.

"Naw, a cat wouldn't come this close to people, would it?" I paused. "Besides, I'd hate to see a cat that could have moved that in one swipe!"

"Well, if it was a man, I wouldn't want to meet him, either," Bruce scoffed, but we both began sneaking quick looks at the clumps of rocks and bushes. There was plenty of cover for anything to hide. This area had always been a popular place with hermits and outlaws.

After a while, Bruce said, "We can't see anything tonight."

"Yeah, let's fix the hole and check it out in the morning," I replied.

We climbed on the roof and tugged the sheetrock back in place. It took both of us to move it. We added a couple more rocks. A bat flew past my head, and I almost backed off the building as I frantically swatted the air with my hat. Bruce started laughing.

"Not funny, Bruce!" I glared at him. "Wait 'til that thing comes and moves your roof again."

Back in the cabin, we moved Bruce's bed next to mine then pretended to sleep the rest of the night. Never had the desert made so much noise before. I had always believed in the stillness of the desert, but that night I imagined every creak as a return of our strange guest. I think I even heard a rat cough.

We never did find out who our mysterious visitor was. There

were no tracks around but ours, and we hadn't walked near the other end of the cabins. Maybe it was a cougar or a man, but I often ask myself if it could have been one of the ancient ones returning to let us know we are not alone in the desert, that we are only beginning to know its secrets. After all, they were there first.

Bob at Hidden Splendor.

NEVER GIVE UP

Shortly after "The Visitor" incident in Hidden Splendor, Junie's family and Bob were staying at the cabin. Bob's nephew Carl Dean was playing around the cabin and fell in a big puddle that had been left behind after the last rainstorm. He was two years old.

When it was dinnertime, Bob and Bruce went looking for Carl Dean. They found him lying face down in the water without a ripple around him. They got him out, and he wasn't breathing at all. Bob started giving him mouth to mouth. After a few minutes, Bruce told Bob that he was gone and it was no good. Bob refused to quit.

Junie took her other two children by the hand and led them into the cabin. Then she knelt down and prayed. That was something she had not done in quite a long time.

A few moments later, Bob felt Carl Dean's hand twitch, and he knew he was going to come back. He kept on until Carl started breathing on his own. Then they all scrambled into the truck, went to the Junction for June and Edith, and headed for the doctor in Green River. Little Carl Dean's eyes would flutter when they spoke to him, but he did not wake up on the way there.

The doctor said they just had to wait for the outcome. There was no telling if Carl Dean would regain consciousness, or if he would have brain damage if he did. Many long hours later, Carl Dean woke up and asked for a drink of water. He had pain in his joints for a while but otherwise was okay.

SPLASH!

Bob held various jobs. Like his dad, he liked to roam and tried his hand at many things. He drove both semis and dump trucks for many years.

He drove truck for Utah Concrete Pipe Company when they were building the Glen Canyon Dam and lived in the small town of Trackyte (which is now underwater in Lake Powell), or sometimes he would stay at Temple Junction. The construction crews had made a cut in the side of the cliff for the trucks to come down, and they built a one-way bridge over the San Juan River. Two cars would fit, but not two semis. The trucks at the bottom were supposed to wait and make sure a truck was not coming down from the top. Since the road was gravel, a loaded semi could not stop on the steep road, so they needed the right-of-way over the bridge.

Bob came over the hill with a full load and saw a truck at the bottom. He figured the other truck would wait, since that's what the rules were, and he started down the steep grade. When he was halfway down the hill, he realized the other truck was headed for the bridge. It was too late to stop; if he tried, the heavy truck would slide and roll over, so he kept on. He and the other driver met on the middle of the bridge. Bob had pulled his truck as far as he dared to the side, and when they passed, he saw the other driver's eyes were as wide as saucers. Their mirrors clipped each other as they passed, but the two trucks did not hit.

Bob heaved a big sigh—what a relief! Then he glanced at his other mirror in time to see his back tires sliding over the edge of the bridge! He started rolling down his window as fast as he could, and that's the last thing he remembered. Next thing he knew, the other semi driver was pulling him out of the river. He was beside himself, apologizing and explaining he had not seen Bob's truck until he was on the bridge. Amazingly, Bob was uninjured, just soaked to the skin. It's a good thing seatbelts were not required back then. That was one time they would not have helped.

The rivers in that part of the country have so much fine sand in them that if something is heavy enough to sink in the sand, it usually can't be pulled back out. The semi and all the pipe are still there; it was too long before they could get a big outfit there to get anything out. The river had swallowed the truck and buried it under the sand.

THE EDSEL

Sometimes, fate is kind. Sometimes, Death reaches out to take lives, and then in a rather fickle way, draws back his hand.

The advertising campaign for the Edsel car was quite impressive. Bob was very proud of the car when he bought it. It had a lot of modern conveniences, one of which was the magical push-button transmission. No more fussing with the clutch.

Bob had married by then and had three small children. He'd taken the kids for a drive with him to pick up his paycheck. They liked to watch the big trucks roll by and see how much progress had been made on the massive Glen Canyon Dam.

On his way to get his paycheck, Bob pulled over in the shade offered by the lee of the cliff. The car was overheating a little, which was not unusual in those days, even for newer cars. The road followed the San Rafael River at that point, and the cattle trail that had clung to the cliff face had been blasted wider to allow for a two-lane road. Little Bobby, Jessie, and David hopped out of the car to stretch their legs. They chucked rocks into the river far below and generally had fun making up things to do until Bob told them to get back in the car, telling them they'd be on their way soon.

Bob went to the back of the car to check on something the kids had spotted at the side of the road. He was looking down at what turned out to be an old leather case when the car began to move on its own.

One of the kids had hit the button on the console to put the car in neutral. Bob's heart plummeted. The car was picking up speed. The car was parked in a curve of the road facing downhill. It was heading straight for the cliff that dropped into the river. Bob said he'd never run so fast in his life. All the windows were down on the car that day, and the kids had not rolled them up.

Bob was screaming at them to push the park button, but they didn't understand his words or the danger they were in. Bob caught up to the car, his legs and lungs screaming, and reached through the window to push a button, any button, on the console. He hit reverse. The car's transmission ground with a shriek and the car sputtered to a stop less than ten feet from the edge of the cliff.

Bob ripped the door open, chucked little Bobby out of the seat, and twisted the steering wheel so they'd be heading away from danger. He wasn't sure if he'd damaged the car, but it started up okay and they drove on. It took more than an hour for Bob's hands to stop shaking.

HITCHHIKERS

Bob was a Democrat, and he loved to debate politics with anyone who would join in. He didn't argue in an offensive way or make the other person feel like an idiot, so a lot of his friends felt okay about arguing with him about his ideas, even if they were Republicans.

When Bob was driving truck for Utah Concrete Pipe Company, the president sent out a written memo that it was now their strict policy that you did not pick up hitchhikers, even if they looked benign. This was right after a couple of truckers were hijacked and killed by men who had been posing as stranded travelers. Most truckers drove in convoys for a while after that incident.

However, it wasn't economical or logical to send truckers out in convoys in the remote stretches of road Bob was often driving. So, he was heading alone for a jobsite in what was called the "Little Sahara" with a load of culvert. He saw two guys at the side of the road with the tire and wheel off their car and stopped to see if he could help out. Bob knew the rules about hitchhikers they had been lectured about but didn't think these two men counted. Both men were well dressed in business suits and were very polite. He found out that they had no water or food and, of course, this was long before cellphones. The wheel on the car was ruined. Even if it had been good, they had no spare tire.

He told them to hop in and he would take them to Delta. On the way to Delta, he found out their ultimate destination was the Salt Lake City Capitol building. One of the men (Bob did not remember his name) said he was the head of federal housing. The other introduced himself as George Romney. Bob didn't recognize either man's name.

Bob told them that once he dropped off his load of culvert, he was going back to Salt Lake to pick up another load, so he might as well take them all the way in. They were very grateful. While they were in Delta, the two men made arrangements for their car to be towed, then they climbed back in Bob's truck with him and had a nice time chatting and talking politics all the way back to the city. Bob dropped them off at the Capitol building and thought no more of it.

About a month later, the president of Utah Concrete Pipe called a meeting of all the crew that was there. He had a letter in his hand from George Romney, Governor of Michigan, stating how grateful he was for the kindness Bob showed him and his companion. The president of the company went on for a while about how good this was for public relations, and he was glad Bob went the extra mile by helping those men out.

After the meeting, the rest of the truck drivers wasted no time cornering Bob and complaining. Why does he get a thank-you from the company president for picking up hitchhikers?!

KEEP YOUR FEET ON SOLID GROUND

It was not a good idea to get on a plane with Bob. He didn't have a very good track record. He was drafted into the Army during the Korean War when he was nineteen. The Army had booked a commercial flight to ship the men from Fort Lewis, Washington, to Fort Hood, Texas, to complete basic training. On the way, they were scheduled to stop for fuel. It was supposed to be a short stop, and the flight attendants told them not to exit the plane. But when they arrived at the fueling station, they started flying in big loops around the base. Finally, the pilot came on the intercom and said they were nearly out of fuel and would have to make an emergency landing. The disembodied voice crackling over the intercom said they had been working on the problem, but the landing gear on the plane would not go down.

Nearly all the passengers were enlisted men. They put their helmets on, gathered their packs into their laps, and hugged them tight. Bob was seated by a window; he could see himself being ripped to shreds when the window blew out and wondered if he'd die of that, or be burned alive, or maybe suffocate when the fire took all the air. Then there was a hideous thump and screech when the belly of the plane slid along the ground. The pilots had figured it would be better if they landed off the runway with the thought that the scrub would be a softer landing than the tarmac. But this was west Texas; the space next to the runway was cactus and gravel, not grass.

Sparks flew past the window, and metal screeched so loud

Bob's ears buzzed the rest of the day. Everyone waited for a spark to ignite the nearly empty gas tanks and blow the plane to smithereens.

The plane hit a berm in the dirt that twisted it sideways and slid it up onto the tarmac. At that point, Bob imagined the plane turning cartwheels.

What struck him most was the silence from all the people in the plane full of men. There is a point beyond fear when you can't even shout.

After an eternity, the plane slid to a halt. People joke about having to "change their shorts" when they get scared, but Bob assured me that was more than true for many of the people on that plane.

They were sent off the plane and into a hanger to get checked out and to clean up. Miraculously, everyone was okay. Then the Army, being the Army, told them to load up into another plane, and they'd be on their way.

Bob was not the only one who flatly refused to get back in a plane that day. He would have preferred a court-martial. They ended up arranging for buses to take them the rest of the way.

Bob lucked out and didn't end up going to Korea during the conflict. He had been doing maintenance on aircraft Hill Air Base when he was drafted. Bob served as a radio communications man in the Army. He also won several medals for his sharpshooting skills.

As a soldier, it wasn't an option not to fly, no matter how uncomfortable it made you. After Fort Hood, he was sent to Fort Benning, Georgia, and then to New Jersey. While he was there, he had taken a lady out for dinner, and they were on the subway when the train stopped and they were told to exit. He found himself in a crowd made up of all colors, sizes, and shapes, and there were more people than he had ever seen in his life, all heading in the same direction like cattle at a stockyard. It was New Year's Eve, and he ended up in Time Square to watch the ball drop.

The problem was, he had a curfew. He got written up for being late back to the barracks. There were gates and guards around Time Square, so he had to stay until it was over.

The next time Bob flew on a plane, he was on TDY (Temporary Duty Yonder) while working at Hill Air Base. They were coming in to land in Tokyo, Japan. The flight had been calm with no turbulence, and most of the men had slept. Bob couldn't talk himself into that, so he and a few of the other men had played poker games with Bob's stack of beat-up cards.

As they approached Japan, the officers on the plane at the back hurried to the front and gathered in a group at the door to the cockpit. They were clearly excited but were talking in whispers with their backs to the plane full of passengers.

It was another case of the plane being almost out of fuel, so they had to land. They landed in Tokyo during an earthquake and felt the plane bounce up and down while the ground rolled underneath them. The tin roofs on the houses they could see out the windows looked like waves on the ocean as the bamboo supports that held them up swayed back and forth, up and down. The struts on the plane caved in from the impact when the ground bucked up beneath it.

It was a tough decision about whether to stay on the plane or risk the ground that day. The worst thing was, Bob knew he'd have no choice but to take a plane back home. After all, there was an ocean in the way, and he was sure Hill Air Base would not pay to send him on a cruise.

JESSIE'S FLIGHT

Bob, Joyce, Jessie, Don, and LaVar (on top, fueling his plane).

Speaking of airplanes, Bob's cousin LaVar—from the Wells clan—flies planes as a hobby and for a living. One of his jobs for many years was following the gas line and checking on its status regularly. The line goes the length of Utah from south to north. Another regular job he had was counting the owls among the cliffs in Canyonlands.

I suppose I should explain about counting owls. Some environmentalists came up with a brilliant plan. They relocated some endangered spotted owls and turned them loose in the Henry Mountains as an attempt to protect the old-growth forest there and keep the logging industry from cutting down the trees. The owls settled in for a short time in the mountains. Then the clever birds took a look around at the high, cold mountains and compared them to the warm cliffs and sandbanks in and around Lake Powell. In less than a year, all the owls had abandoned the Henry Mountains and moved to the canyons. So, the plan to protect the forest was a fail, but the endangered owls thrived in the cliffs.

Each owl had a band on its leg that transmitted a unique signal. LaVar would fly around the cliffs, locate each owl, and mark where it was found. If the band didn't move for a few days, a ranger would hike to the site and find out if the owl was nesting or had died.

LaVar is a brave man. Even knowing Bob's dismal track record when it came to flying, he persisted asking until he talked Bob into going for a ride in his plane. After a handful of trips, Bob got so he wasn't quite as uncomfortable in a plane as he used to be.

LaVar had a few passengers on the plane with him one time, and Bob's daughter Jessie was with them. She isn't too keen on flying either, but she took LaVar up on his offer to fly through Canyonlands and get a bird's-eye view of that breathtaking country while he counted owls.

As they approached the plane, Bob pointed out the duct tape that adorned one of the small plane's wings. LaVar said not to worry. There was nothing wrong with the structure of the plane, just the skin was peeling off in that place, and he hadn't had a chance to get it fixed.

Bob and Jessie exchanged a look, but they didn't want to back out of this rare chance, so they climbed in. Jessie then noted that her seatbelt didn't have a matching side. There was nothing to clip it into. LaVar told her not to worry. The weather was good, so they would have no turbulence. She and Bob exchanged another look.

Once they were out over the canyons, both Bob and Jessie forgot their fears. They had become mesmerized by the amazing vistas and vermillion cliffs. They had even counted a couple of owls. Jessie asked how fast they were going, and LaVar's reply made her comment, "It doesn't seem like we're going that fast." LaVar grinned, then slid the plane over so they were flying parallel to a towering cliff.

Jessie screamed, and since she didn't have a seatbelt, she jumped up and grabbed Bob around the head.

Everyone got a good chuckle out of that. Then LaVar thought he'd have some more fun. He tipped the nose of the plane up and gunned the engines into a climb so they were looking at the beautiful desert sky with its unique shade of blue. There weren't even any clouds. A perfect day for flying. Then LaVar tipped the nose down.

The lack of gravity at that moment lifted them out of their seats. Bob didn't go far because his seatbelt had both parts. Jessie came clear out of her seat. She screamed loud enough that time to make it echo in the tiny cockpit, and she grabbed the first thing she could find to hang onto: Bob's head. She hugged him so tight he couldn't see a thing. Then the brief moment of no gravity was over, and she settled onto her seat. It took a minute or two for her to get enough breath to start chewing LaVar out.

LaVar pretended he didn't know what she was upset about. Jessie had been too busy hollering to notice they were in another climb. She shouted about making them float, and LaVar said, "Oh, you mean like this?" And he dropped the nose again.

She survived the trip, and when they disembarked back on solid ground, they found LaVar had been telling them the truth. The duct tape hadn't moved at all during their flight.

FIRE

In the summer of 1969, the movie *Vanishing Point* was filmed, and they used Temple Junction in one of the scenes, so if you're curious, you can see the place on film.

There are times when you do have to throw in the towel. It was not an easy feat getting the Junction going. While building the bar, the family lived in tents and had to wrap themselves in blankets, including their heads, because the mice that abound in that sandy country would crawl around on them in the night. If it wasn't mice, it was snakes.

The wind blew constantly and, before going to bed, they had to carry their blankets outside the wall tent and shake the sand off. Plus, it was *cold* at night. The desert air does not hold the heat in. Imagine their relief when they were able to finish the doors and windows on the house behind the bar and could live without critters sharing their tent.

Eventually, the place was going strong. There were many buildings, and business was good enough that they had a large generator plus several big coolers to keep up with demand in the café and bar.

June, Bob, and the rest of the family built the place by hand. None of them had been taught how to build; they just figured it out as they went, including the wiring. June had decided when they were shut down for Labor Day that he would do the wiring right. He took some sheetrock down on Sunday while the family went to town for supplies and to see a movie.

June was taking a break reading and kept seeing a light, but he thought it was the cars going by on the highway. By the time he realized it was a fire, it was too late. He tried to put out the fire himself. He used the water pumps until they ran dry, and the well. About then, the family came back, but they could not save anything, even if they had gone to Hanksville for the fire department.

Their supplier had been insured, but the buildings were not, so Temple Junction and June's dream of finishing life with a successful business out on the desert he loved so much was gone.

It was cancer that took June's life. It was most likely caused by all those years mining uranium. Near the end, the family brought him home instead of making him stay in the hospital. On the night he died, Edith was holding his hand, and the music box that was sitting across the room began to play. No one was near it or could explain why it would do that. He died on January 3rd at 5:30, the exact day and time Rosalee died forty years earlier.

PART TWO: ADVENTURES WITH HORSES

THE OLD RANCH

The main house with the washtub still on the wall.

The actual name of the ranch when Alma Marsing owned it was the Red Cliff Ranch, but by the time I showed up on the scene and began going on trips in there with Bob, it was called the Old Ranch. It lies on the Price River in central Utah. The buildings are still there, although now the tamarisk is tall enough that you can't see them until you're up close, and the dirt has fallen through the cedar poles on the roofs. Sand and packrat nests vie for space inside the buildings.

It was a large and prosperous ranch in the first two decades of the 1900s. Then Alma's wife Annabelle died and took the wind out of Alma's sails. He did remarry, but his new wife's kids were lazy and didn't want to do the kind of hard work a ranch requires. Alma's own children had married and moved away by then. The drought had dried up the country enough that the river changed course and took out the hay fields, turning the green fields into sandbanks and gullies. Eventually, Alma divorced his second wife and let the desert claim the ranch.

Many years later, in the 1970s, Bob's uncle Doug took him into the ranch by way of the Ivy Place. It was an abandoned homestead built after the narrow-gauge railroad project in that area was scrapped. After that, Bob started taking his friends who had horses on trips to the ranch. Sometimes as many as fifteen riders and almost as many truck and camper rigs would trail through the desert following Bob.

There are always adventures on the long ride into the ranch, especially at the river crossings. Some stories stand out more than others. I've tried to describe the ones we like to retell the most in this section.

SPOOKY OLD ALICE

One of the first trips Bob took into the Old Ranch was with a bunch of friends who worked with him at Hill Air Base (everyone around here just calls it "Hill"). One of those was Jack Heinz. He was a World War II veteran who served as a driver for Patton and liked to say the movie got everything about him right except his voice. Patton had a "girlie" voice, as Jack put it. Jack lost his right arm in the Battle of the Bulge. He only had about eight inches of it left below the shoulder joint. He and his Jeep were hit with shrapnel. Even years later, he still had pieces of metal that would pop up under his skin.

When Bob was arranging a trip into the ranch, Jack wanted to go, but he didn't have a horse. Bob's chariot racing partner at the time was Bob Folkman. He said he would lend Jack a horse.

The closest the trailers and trucks could get to the ranch was a place named the Old Ivy Place. It lay alongside Icelander Wash and was made from the leftover railroad ties from the narrow-gauge tracks. There were about six rigs that time. They pulled their campers and trailers around in a circle in front of the old homestead and corrals that made up the Ivy Place and unloaded.

They decided a good Dutch oven dinner would be a great thing to come back to, so before they rode out, they dug a hole and put some hot coals in it. They filled a Dutch oven with roast, carrots, potatoes, and broth. Then they put the lid on the oven and more hot coals on top. They buried it so some coyote wouldn't dig it up or tip it over while they were gone. Everyone's mouths watered, thinking of the supper that awaited them when they returned.

Then they started saddling up. Jack liked to do things for himself, and he was familiar with horses and riding, so they all left him to it. The horse Folkman loaned Jack was a mare whose nickname was "Spooky Old Alice." I don't think anyone remembers her true registered name anymore. I wonder now if Bob Folkman lent him that horse to see what would happen, or if her name was just a fluke.

Anyway, once they had them all saddled, Bob asked Jack if he'd like some help putting her bridle on. Jack said, "No, I've got it."

Jack usually went without his artificial arm, but for the ride, he put it on. It was a simple arm with a hook at the end, nothing fancy. Jack placed the headstall (the top of the bridle) on the hook and lifted it up to pull it over Alice's ears. About the time he settled it on her head and moved to fasten the throat latch on (the small strap that goes around the horse's throat), the hook on his artificial arm turned over and squeaked. Old Alice thought that sounded strange, so she jumped a little and scooted sideways. When she did that, the hook on Jack's arm slid under her halter.

That meant Jack's artificial arm was hooked onto the top of the mare's halter between her ears. Alice sidled sideways even faster, and Jack had no choice but to follow her. Now the mare was *really* scared. This stranger had grabbed her by the head and was hanging on! She started running sideways, and Jack had a time of it keeping his feet under him. Alice gave up on going sideways and started spinning in a circle, trying to get away from the scary stranger. Jack's feet left the earth, and he was hanging straight out in midair with his arm still hooked on the halter.

She spun around several times, fast enough that Jack was flat-out sideways. Finally, the harness that held his arm on gave way, ripped the sleeve off his shirt as it went, and Jack landed in a heap several feet away from the mare.

Spooky Old Alice now had the arm hanging from her halter. In her mind, she still hadn't gotten away from that scary thing, so she thought she'd try running away from it. She took off at top speed (this mare had a AAA speed index, which meant she was no slouch when it came to running) up a steep hill and ran out of steam at the top. She stood at the top, outlined by the morning sun, and snorted at that thing hanging from her head.

It was awhile before anyone could go get her. They were all doubled over laughing too hard to be of any help to her or Jack. No one, including Jack, could even breathe.

Both Jack and Alice came out of it okay. Jack took it all in stride; he had a great sense of humor. They carried on and rode to the ranch, but Jack had to go without his arm. No one had any leather straps that would fix it.

They were all tuckered out when they got back. It's a long, hot ride. From the Ivy Place, it's about a thirty-mile ride to go to the ranch and back. They stripped the tack off the horses and got them fed and watered. The whole time, they were thinking of how good dinner was going to taste. Finally, the horses were all settled in, and they dug up the Dutch oven.

They had overdone the hot coals. The only things in the oven were bits of meat and vegetables, charred black and hard as a rock.

It was canned goods for dinner that night.

MUTTON WITHERS

Bob, Sis, and Missy.

When Bob's boy David rode into the ranch the first time, Bob mentioned that Joyce would like to see it too. David said, "The only way you'll get Joyce in there is to float her in."

Mom didn't ride horses, and David figured the ride was too much for someone not used to rough riding. The problem was, he'd said it within earshot of Mom. She announced she was going to ride in there "Come hell or high water!"

When Bob realized Mom was serious about riding into the Old Ranch, he traded his friend a two-year-old colt we had for a little buckskin mare named Sis. She was thin when we got her, but soon became "round as a barrel" in horse-speak, which is a creative way to say "fat." One of Bob's favorite sayings when speaking about horses was "fat's a pretty color." Horses do look better when they're round and not too slim.

Sis also had mutton withers. You know that bump at the base of your neck that the tag on your shirt rubs, and it drives you nuts? That's the same bone on a horse called the "withers." I've never found anyone who knows where that word came from. Anyway, it's the big bump at the base of a horse's neck. It's handy for keeping your saddle from sliding sideways. Sheep don't have withers, hence the term "mutton withers"—a horse who has little or no withers. What all that means is that they don't hold a saddle on very well.

On my first trip into the Old Ranch, Bob rode Mom's little buckskin mare, and I rode a two-year-old colt named Special. About halfway to the ranch, when you come in from the Old Ivy Place, there are sand gullies that you have to go up, down, and around. They are deep enough that at the bottom of the gullies that you can't see over the top, even on a horse. They go on for a good mile or so, and when we were done winding our way through, Special was pretty tired. We stopped so he could take a breather. He was standing there trying to catch his breath. We were sideways to the wind. It was warm and dry, and I wore hard contacts. The wind took my contact and flipped it right out of my eye.

I blame my parents for my very bad eyesight. I got glasses in third grade and got contacts when I was twelve. I knew there was little or no chance I could find it, but I got off Special anyway and looked around under Sis since that's the way the wind would have blown it. It was lying on the sand right under her belly! Wonders never cease.

I stuck it in my mouth and sucked on it and looked up while I did. Bob's cinch (the strap that holds the saddle on the horse) was hanging loose about two inches off the mare's belly. He had a lightning buckle on the cinch, and it had come undone. Her hair was dry under the cinch. That meant it had been undone for quite some time.

Keeping a saddle on that mare was always a challenge for me, even with the saddle on tight. But Bob had ridden up and down gullies and sandhills, and his saddle hadn't even moved.

Bob was annoyed with himself that he hadn't noticed. I was amazed.

HUMBLE PIE

Jessie is Bob's daughter, and David is his youngest son. Bob invited them down to ride into the Old Ranch with us on my second trip in. It was just us four. We planned to ride to the ranch, camp the night, and ride back out the next day. Jessie is older than I am by four years, and David is one year older. On that trip, we were all teenagers.

When riding in from the Old Ivy Place, there are five river crossings. You can only cross in certain spots because the riverbanks are too steep everywhere else. The river crossings are the exciting part of the ride. Someone usually gets soaked at least once at the river.

We had made it to the last crossing on the way in. I had been there the year before, but the river was running faster and wilder this time. Bob sent David across first since he was on Sis, who was the most reliable horse we had. He told him to head for a sandbank over on the other side that looked like a bit of a leap, but one a horse could make. Sis, being a game horse, jumped up on the bank with her front legs, but the water had undercut the bank underneath, so she tipped over backwards into the river. She flipped back over, shook her head, and walked back across to us. David was still standing on the other side of the river in water past his waist, looking forlorn, until Jessie hollered at him, "Well, come on back." He sloshed across back to us.

I rode out into the river to get David's sleeping bag, which was floating away downstream. Hotshot, even though he was only a three-year-old colt, loved water, so he thought the river was great.

I brought the sleeping bag back then started arguing with Bob. I didn't understand why we didn't just cross a little way upstream where we had crossed the year before. Bob said, "We can't cross there this year." Being a teenager, who therefore knew *everything*, I said, "Well, I'm going to try it."

I rode Hotshot out into the middle of the river. At that point, the water was stirrup high. Hotshot stopped since the horse was smarter than I was. Bob said in a wry tone, "I wouldn't go any farther."

I ignored him and spurred Hotshot on. He willingly stepped forward. We went underwater all the way to my hat. I grabbed for it and caught it as we popped back up. I still had the reins in my hands, so as Hotshot turned around to go back to the horses, I grabbed the saddle, too. I had just discovered you can't swim with heavy leather chaps on. Hotshot dragged me to the bank, unfazed. He thought it was a nice day for a swim.

Bob was a kind man. Neither he nor his kids said, "I told you so."

We gave up on riding in the final leg to the ranch that day. We rode back to Newkirk's cabin, where there were some old corrals, and set up camp there.

Alma would get people to settle near the ranch, build them a cabin, and get them to make a claim with the state for that section of land. Then Alma would run cattle and grow hay on it. Newkirk was a crazy old man who would sometimes forget who Alma and his kids were and would chase them away from the cabin with his pitchfork. That's how that part of the ranch got the name Newkirk's Cabin. It lay in a long, flat area that still had the hay derrick and hay corral on it when we first rode in. Many years later, the river took out even more of the former fields, and it took the derrick, too.

A hay derrick, if you've never seen one, looks like a tripod with a long arm hanging from the top. It was made to swing the hay from the wagon bed to the haystack. A corral was always built around the hay derrick so the cattle and horses would stay out. In free-range country, it's the hay that's in corrals, not the critters.

On that ride, it was hot enough that David and I dried off fairly

104

quickly, but we had sand and salt in our hair and clothes for the rest of the day. Poor David was the worst off. He had rolled it tight, but his sleeping bag was still half soaked.

That night as we tried to get to sleep, David kept whispering, "Jessie, what was that?" There were bats flying around and other weird noises since we weren't used to nights out there. One bat even landed on David's sleeping bag. I could hear Bob chuckle and Jessie sigh. At about midnight, there was an awful noise, and David sat straight up. Mom's mare had started to snore. If you've never heard a horse snore, it's loud. Sounds a little like a lion roaring. I can't speak for the others, but I didn't get any sleep.

The next day, we walked the last mile to the ranch on foot. Although heights have never bothered me, I discovered that day that I get vertigo when I'm up high and water is moving down below, so I crawled around the edge of the cliff. The trail used to be a wagon road, but it has eroded away, so it is now only about three feet wide. The river flows by almost one hundred feet down.

We stayed at the ranch for a couple of hours. It was only my second time there, and Jessie and David hadn't been there before. When we were done wandering through the old buildings, we went back and saddled up. Luckily, the horses hadn't broken out of our makeshift corral.

Old cowboys know things that they don't put in books. We had been riding for quite a while and had come up to yet another narrow trail along a cliff. Bob was in front, and he suddenly slapped Buddy on the hip with his reins. I was just about to ask him what that was for since I didn't see Buddy do anything wrong when Bob turned his head and said, "Wake your horse up and tell Jessie and Dave to do the same."

I slapped Hotshot with the reins then started to turn my head. I got as far as "Wake" when Special's hind legs fell off the cliff. Both he and Jessie started sliding down the hill. Jessie was scrambling, clinging to rocks and brush. I found out that horses can crawl, too, because that's what Special did. He crawled back up onto the trail alongside Jessie. Everyone was awake then!

We took people into the ranch almost every year, sometimes as many as fifteen at a time, but usually only six or so. Bob rarely had

105

any trouble. In fact, there were only two times he had any problems that I remember, both when riding Buddy.

THE SUBMARINE

Bob and Buddy, ready to cross the Price River.

On that same trip with David and Jessie, before I ate humble pie, we had come to the first river crossing. Bob sent David over first on Sis. Being a good old broke horse, she stepped down into the river and walked to the sandbar to wait for Jessie and me to cross. We were both on colts. Special had been to the ranch the previous year, so he took a few big gulps of water and then splashed across to wait alongside David and Sis.

I was on Hotshot. He tended to hurry through things rather than thinking them through. He had never seen a river before, but his stablemate Special was on the other side, and he wanted to get to him. He gathered all four feet on the rock on the bank and leaped out as far as he could into the river.

He landed with a tremendous splash and soaked Jessie with the spray. Even David got sprinkled, although his mare was on the far side of Special.

Jessie gasped in shock when the cold water hit her and chewed me out while David and Bob laughed, and I mumbled an apology. Then we turned around to watch Bob cross the river. Buddy was still staring at the stupid colts and the weird people laughing. So, when Bob asked him to go, he didn't look down. He just took a step ahead.

Bob had some phrases he used when referring to Buddy. One was "He's a good, honest horse." Another was "He has lots of try" (meaning he would give you his all no matter what you asked him to do). The third was "He's not the brightest pebble." Buddy was not too smart. Just smart enough to do what was asked, but he didn't come up with much in the way of his own ideas.

On that riverbank, Buddy wasn't prepared to step off into water. Bob asked him to go, so he went, and his foot just kept going down . . . into three feet of water. He stumbled and almost fell to his knees. He was fairly sure-footed and caught himself from rolling all the way over, but by then his head was completely underwater. We could see his head, the water was so clear, and bubbles boiled out of his nose like a submarine about to surface.

Bob was making little "Ah, ah, ah" noises from the cold water that washed over the pommel of his saddle. He pulled at the slick reins and cussed and kept spluttering from the sudden cold. Jessie, David, and I almost fell off our horses laughing.

Old Buddy stumbled forward, still trying to keep his feet, and finally popped his head back up. He tilted his head sideways with both ears hanging down since they had water in them. I had never seen anything that looked so forlorn and funny at the same time. He shook his head, and one wet rein slipped out of Bob's hands. It didn't matter, though. By then, Buddy was standing still, wondering what happened, and Bob was cussing about everything being wet—pants, chaps, saddle, pads . . . The only thing not wet was his lunch and sleeping bag. The top of Buddy's haunches (butt) hadn't gone under, and Bob's body had blocked the water from washing that way.

Finally, Bob had to laugh too, especially at the expression on Buddy's face. The gelding kept shaking his head to try to get the water out of his ears, tilting his head sideways, ears hanging, looking confused.

My ribs hurt by the time Bob and Buddy joined us on the sandbar.

I don't think Buddy ever figured out why he'd gotten a dunking. But at the next river crossing, he stepped right in like the "good, honest horse" he was. He did watch his feet that time, though.

Of the four of us, Jessie was the only one who stayed dry the whole trip.

YER GOIN' IN THE RIVER!

Sometimes, advice just isn't helpful.

On another trip to the Old Ranch, I was riding our two-year-old Paint stallion. Stud colts are a pain in the you-know-what, and Patches was no exception. He was full of himself as we started out: snorting and blowing, squealing at the strange horses he'd never met, trying to impress them. There was quite a crowd with us; at least a dozen riders. I kept having to take Patches off to the side to try to keep him from bothering the other riders.

We rode up the long hill from the Ivy Place and down the other side toward the river. When we got near the river, there were sandbanks, and we had to wind our way down. Patches was being quite a handful and wasn't about to pay attention to his rider. I was getting more than frustrated at him.

The colt was finding out that this kind of country was a lot harder to navigate than the arena and hillside at home, and he didn't trust me enough to listen to anything I tried to get him to do. At that time, I was too stubborn to get off and lead him.

Bob was leading the way on Buddy, and I was following Mom, who was on Tonto, hoping the colt would follow that horse and go where he went.

He didn't.

When Tonto cut around a sandbank and stopped, Patches figured it would be easier to jump down to where Tonto was rather than going around the sandbank like I asked him to.

Tonto was standing right next to the river. But Patches could not know that. The tamarisk was taller than us, even on horseback.

Patches leaped out at the same time I yelled, "Whoa!"

Bob, handing out absolutely unhelpful advice, hollered, "Yer goin' in the river!"

I thought, "No kidding!" The colt, having jumped down like that, had too much momentum to stop himself and had to keep going. Luckily, he saw the sagebrush at his feet and made a second leap over that instead of flipping over.

We sailed out into midair. I had enough time during the flight to consider leaping clear of the colt, just in case. And even more time to decide that I wanted him to hit whatever we hit first. I took my feet out of the stirrups but hung on to the saddle horn.

After an eternity, we landed in water up to the colt's chest. The splash soaked me and Patches, and the huge rocks on either side of us. The rocks stood out of the water and would have crushed Patches or me both if that's what he had landed on instead of water.

I fell off when we landed and lunged for the black cowboy hat I had been wearing, but it was out of reach. It floated down the river and out of sight. It belonged in that country anyway—it had been June's hat.

I gathered up Patches' reins and waded down the river a ways to find a place for us to get out. It took a while for the rest of them to cross the river, where sane people would go, and join us.

Patches was quite humble for the rest of the ride. He barely even nickered at anyone. And ever after that, when I said "whoa," he stopped. I think he thought I'd thrown him in that river on purpose.

RIVER CROSSINGS

Speaking of rivers, as I mentioned before, that's usually where the excitement is.

Thoroughbreds are an interesting breed. Thoroughbred, with a capital T, is the name of a breed of horse, as opposed to thoroughbred, which means well-bred. Thoroughbreds often qualify under both terms. They are incredibly brave if they trust their rider, and unbelievably chicken if they don't. For most of them, being racehorse bred, they figure the faster they go, the better things will be. In other words, they tend to hurry through the scary parts.

Rivers are usually frightening for horses. They can't see where they are putting their feet. So is being left behind. Predators *eat* stragglers, you know.

One time we were coming back from the ranch, and my nephew Jeremy was on old Easy. Easy was an ex-racehorse, but his training as a racehorse had either been exceptional, or he was just naturally easygoing like his name implied. He raced for thirteen years, most of it on the chariots, and he even won the Iron Horse Award from the Quarter Horse Association for his long years of racing. But little kids could ride him around with a simple plain ring snaffle bridle on, and they'd be safe. I boarded him for a friend, and they let us use him. Jeremy had borrowed him so he could ride in and see the Old Ranch in person.

It was quite windy and a little cold that day. We were glad to be heading back. It was about a three-foot drop down into the river on that side. Old Easy plopped his front feet down in the water and left his hind end up on the bank. He figured it was a good time to get a drink. Jeremy tried to pull his head up so he would at least have all four feet in the river, but Easy ignored him. They were tilted at a steep angle, and I was glad old Easy had good withers for keeping a saddle on.

My oldest daughter, Jennifer, was behind him on a big gray Thoroughbred we had for a little while. He was okay, but his training as a racehorse had not been that good, and he had issues we had been working on sorting out. We had only had him for a couple months. He was excited that we were finally going in the right direction—toward the horse trailers. He didn't want to slow down for anything, even the river, and he was ignoring Jennifer. They were at the back of the line because she had been arguing with him about *walking*, not *jigging*. He wasn't paying much attention to what she wanted. About the time they got within fifty yards of the river, being a typical racehorse, he decided crossing the river would be better if he went *faster*.

That big gray gelding was even taller and heavier than old Easy was. He started on a long trot and ignored Jennifer pulling on those reins. When they came to Easy standing there with his butt in the air, he jumped right on over both Easy *and* Jeremy.

Jennifer and the horse landed in belly-deep water about halfway across the Price River, splashed water for yards around them, and soaked Easy and Jeremy. The big gray kept on going until he came to the deep, wet sand on the other side where the other horses were gathered. He was tired by then and figured he was safe since he was back with the herd. Jennifer showed those of us gathered there that she knew some words not spoken in church.

***

That story brings me to another one on the same trip.

Jessie has good horses of her own. She had hauled one of her good broke horses down for her grandson to ride, and she was riding Blondie. Blondie was only four and had never been to the desert. Green horses on desert rides are usually a good recipe for some kind of disaster (or a fun story, depending on your

113

perspective). Besides, there's a reason Blondie had that nickname. She was sweet but not the brightest, and she tended to not watch her feet too well.

Although Blondie had never seen a river, she had gone in okay on the way to the ranch. The crossing on that side starts out with mud, then shallows, and then ends with them jumping up a bank. By the time they realize they're in a river, they're almost all the way over, so most horses don't object going that direction. The way back is a different story. They have to step off a steep bank from dry ground and down into the river. Most colts object to that. Blondie was no exception. She didn't want to go in. Jessie could have coaxed her in eventually, but the wind was brisk and cold, and we were all tired.

Jack (this is a different Jack, not Jack Heinz—Jack Fox and his wife, Debbie, have been with us on almost all the rides to the Old Ranch) rode over on his gelding and dallied Jessie's lead rope to his saddle. Unfortunately, Jessie stayed in the saddle instead of getting off. Blondie didn't fold up and fall in like some horses would. She did attempt to jump down, but she stumbled when Jack's horse pulled her in. She pitched forward when her feet hit the gravel under the water, and she flipped Jessie off over her head. Blondie emerged with her ears hanging sideways, full of water like Buddy that one time.

Jessie stood up in the middle of the river, soaked to the skin. The river was about waist deep where she was standing. She picked up Blondie's reins and sloshed across to the other side while Jack mumbled his apologies. He was surprised Blondie hadn't kept her feet. Even when pulled in that way, most horses do.

On the far side, Jessie was standing in deep mud, trying to wring out her clothes while the wind made her teeth chatter. She was balancing on one foot, dumping water out of her boots, and leaning on Blondie. About that time, that big gray horse jumped over Easy and came galloping straight toward Jessie. His big feet slapping the mud spooked the horses. They couldn't see what was coming at them; the brush was too high. When he burst out of the brush, he was only a couple of strides from Jessie.

Jessie watched him come and figured she was going to get

squished, and it would just top off her day. There was no way she could get out of the big gray's way with her feet up to the ankles in mud. But he stopped when he got next to Blondie, and she only got a little mud splashed on her.

Jeremy, and especially Jessie, were frozen like popsicles by the time we got to the trailers.

SAGE ADVICE

We took several people into the ranch who hadn't ridden in that type of country before, and some hadn't ridden horses much at all. I started telling them, "Do what Bob does, go where he goes, and get off when he gets off." Those who followed that idiom never got in a wreck on their ride, but many who did not found themselves dumped off in either the river or a sand gully.

The ride to the ranch isn't for amateurs. The country is too rough. I watched Bob save a couple of people from serious injury or death more than once, and I don't think they were even aware of the danger they were in. Like the time I ate humble pie and took a dunking in the river, it was always when they *didn't* listen to what Bob had to say. He knew all kinds of little things to save yourself trouble when riding.

For instance, don't cross the railroad tracks where they are embedded in the asphalt; cross over on the side where the gravel is. Now, you might get away with it a few dozen times, but there will be that one time when your horse's hoof hits that metal rail and it tilts their hoof back, and now their shoe is stuck in the tracks. The least of that problem is a pulled shoe. You can imagine what the worst is.

Another is: When going up a steep hill, lean forward, don't lean back and pull on the saddle horn; you'll tip your horse over. One of the most hazardous things that can happen to a rider is their horse flipping over backwards. The saddle horn often hits them in the chest and crushes it, or their head bounces off the ground—not too good for the rider in either case.

The river often changed our plans. On one trip, when several of the wives of Bob's friends came along, we had to ride up a steep sandbank flanked by tall tamarisk because the river had cut off the trail. One of the wives was riding a big bay gelding named King. He was the "good as gold" type of horse (that's Bob-speak for a horse you can put anyone one, and they'll take care of them). But a horse can't win over gravity.

Bob had dismounted to find his glasses. While going up the bank, Buddy had flipped his head, and his mane caught Bob's glasses. They flew off into the tamarisk. He had to look for quite a while to find them, and when he did, one of the lenses was broken.

He cussed for a little bit. Then, he told me later, something told him to stay there and help the others go up the bank instead of getting back on. The next rider up was one of the wives on King. She was more than a little nervous—that sandbank was intimidating. She was hanging onto the saddle horn with all she had and leaning back. Bob hollered at her to lean forward, but she didn't—or couldn't—do what he said. Sometimes, fear keeps people from being able to move.

About the time the horse stepped past Bob, gravity took his front feet off the bank, since her weight pulling the wrong direction was too much for him, and they started to tip over. Bob grabbed her arm and jerked her off King before the big bay could land on top of her. The horse kept going over and ended up rolling down the bank, luckily without his rider. He stood up at the bottom of the hill and shook the sand off. She and King came through the ordeal dusty, but otherwise just fine.

APACHE

Apache and Otis tied to the high line, waiting for another adventure.

Most horses are leery of stepping into water and have to be trained to trust their riders enough to do it. Horses are prey for other animals. Putting their feet into something that might trap them, or that they can't see the bottom of, or that seems to be moving, doesn't seem like a good idea to them.

Jasmine started helping me at the barn when she was twelve. She was one of the 4-H kids I taught. Her mom bought her a little yearling mustang, and she started doing chores and generally assisting me with barn stuff to help pay for his board and training.

When Apache was four, we took him and Jasmine down to the

desert with the usual crowd. By then, we had stopped going into the ranch from the Ivy Place and went in by going down Stove Gulch. That way in, there is only one river crossing.

Apache was not keen on water. Even in his own corral at home, he would avoid the puddles. When we got to the river, he didn't give too much of a fuss, so we thought maybe, as seems to be the case for many horses, rivers weren't as scary as puddles.

On the way back was a different story. Apache was never in a hurry and this day was no exception. He was at the back of the line when we got to the river. We all went across and then looked back. Apache was not about to step down into that river. He made it clear he was perfectly happy on the other side, thank you.

This was the same place where Blondie and Jessie were dragged in a few years later.

Bob suggested we ride away through the tamarisk, where Apache wouldn't be able to see us. It often works to motivate another horse to follow if they think they're getting left behind. Well, that didn't work. Apache watched us go and didn't even whinny.

We went back to the riverbank, and Jasmine tried some more to get him to step down. It is quite a drop into the river, about three feet down, so they have to sort of jump in. He could see no good reason to jump down into water from perfectly dry land.

There was no way Jasmine was going to persuade that horse to go in. Bob rode over on Caches and had Jasmine tie Apache's reins up so they wouldn't dangle, then left the lead rope hanging. Jasmine jumped on behind Bob, and he took her across the river. Still Apache, the lone horse on the other side now, would not follow us.

Bev rode her little mare, Ginger, across the river, snagged Apache's lead rope, and dallied it to her saddle horn with a couple of twists. When she started back across, Apache could not outpull that little mare, especially with her lower down than him. He still refused to take a step. Instead, he let the mare drag him into the river. He kept his hooves on the bank as long as he could and just folded up and fell in.

Jasmine is smarter than most. I know I would have stayed on

the horse and waited to see what would happen and gotten a good dunking for it.

After that, Apache would cross water when asked. He didn't like it, but he'd do it without protest.

***

A few years later, we were riding up in Franklin Basin. The river there is ice cold and clear, as opposed to the usually lazy, sand-filled Price River where we cross going into the Old Ranch. Kaytee was there on her horse Badger, who was only three. Badger had never crossed a river before, and he didn't want to go in. I was on a colt too, so he was no good for helping Badger out, and none of us wanted to wade in the freezing water.

I traded Jasmine for Apache and rode him over to Badger. Apache waited patiently, standing quietly in ice water up to his knees while Kaytee and I persuaded Badger to step into the water. Eventually, he did, and like a gentleman, Apache ponied the colt over to the other bank.

As soon as we were all on dry land, Apache reached over and struck the colt's neck, just like a snake. He got a mouthful of Badger's mane and shook him. Take that for making him wade in a river!

WHITE AS A SHEET

Bob didn't outright lie, not to hurt anyone, but he could stretch the truth a little. Two of his pet phrases concerning the desert, I learned after some experience, were not even remotely true. One was "It's a good road." The other was "It's about five miles."

The thing that amazed me was that it was usually the same crowd that followed Bob across the desert, and we all fell for the "It's a good road" every time. Bob liked to take a camper on top of his pickup so he could pull his horse trailer behind. Those desert roads were often "tippy," and when it rained, they were slippery—especially the greenish-gray dirt you find in many spots, like down by the Ivy Place. The country switches from red sand to gray-green limestone clay at random. It makes for some interesting roads sometimes.

***

One time, it had rained all day the day we rode into the Old Ranch. On that trip, it was just Bob, me, and Jack and Debbie Fox. The road was *slick* from the rain. Besides, it wasn't a road for a horse trailer, maybe a four-wheeler, but sane people would not take a horse trailer and camper—only Bob and us idiots who followed him would.

We came to a stretch where the road clung to the side of the hill, and there was only space and rocks on the other side. The road is barely as wide as a pickup anyway. There was a spot where it had washed out. Bob and Jack worked on the bad spot for a few minutes while Debbie and I unloaded the horses. Bob sent Jack on ahead since his truck that year didn't have a camper on it. Jack was a ranch hand too and knew how to drive on roads that aren't really roads. He made it up the hill. Then it was Bob's turn.

You know that phrase "White as a sheet"? Well, I got to see someone do that on that day.

Debbie and I rode our horses bareback and ponied the others up the hill. I was facing away from the road, listening to Jack and Bob holler instructions to each other, and then all the blood drained out of Debbie's face, and she literally looked white as a sheet. I spun my horse around in time to see the truck and camper on two wheels, tilting sideways! Calm as could be, Bob twisted the steering wheel, and the truck settled back down on all four tires.

Jack added more rocks and red sand to the pile, and Bob coaxed the truck and trailer up the hill.

After that trip, if it rained, I refused to ride in the truck until we were out of those hills. I'd rather get a sore butt riding bareback.

RAMBLES

One year, Bob's cousin LaVar took us down for an overnight trip to the Roost. That's the name the locals gave to a stretch of the desert along both sides of the Dirty Devil River. There was quite a string of us riders that time. I was riding BC, who started the ride out by bucking until all the overnight supplies my friend Becki and I had put in my pommel bags were scattered on the ground. I hadn't even tried to get on yet.

BC was only three, and she was all mare. She made her opinion known about *everything*, and she was usually in a bad mood. A friend of Bob's named Duane had brought his leopard-spotted mule, and BC let the mule know she'd take a chunk of hide out of him if he even thought of getting near her. The mule was unfazed; he ignored BC.

Mom was riding good old Tonto, Bob was on Buddy as usual, and Jessie was on Rambles. She was a three-year-old buckskin we had sold to Jessie the year before. It was the first trip to the desert for BC and Rambles.

The ride started out with alternating spots of sandbanks and slick rock. BC may have been ornery, but she was smart, too. When it came to slick rock (slick rock is the term the locals use for the stretches of sandstone slabs in the desert), she soon sought out the spotted mule and followed right behind him. Mules are confident and sure-footed, and she caught on to that, so she didn't have too hard of a time with the slick rock. Rambles seemed to be doing okay too, at first.

LaVar raised cattle down in that country, so his little Arab mare was used to that kind of riding, and he led the way. Most of it was easy going until we got to the river. We had to wind our way down the side of a cliff to get to the stretch of sand that lay between the cliff and the Dirty Devil River (it is appropriately named, by the way). The cliff face was all slick rock and very steep. LaVar rode his little mare down, and Duane followed on his mule, but most of the rest of us got off. Our horses were not quite up to packing a rider down that cliff face.

It was too steep to be safe leading the horses down either, so the first few to go tied their reins up to the saddle horn and turned their horses loose so they could make their way down the trail on their own. Then they would join up with the other horses and riders at the bottom.

Jessie was in the middle of the string of riders, and four of us were behind her. She tied her reins up and showed Rambles the trail, then turned her loose, assuming she would follow like the other horses had.

Colts are known for not being too bright. They often make dumb decisions, just like a lot of teenagers.

I guess I should explain that, in our part of the country, the word "colt" means any horse younger than four, even if it's a filly. A young male horse that is uncut is called a "horse colt." It's like "cows," which are actually female cattle, but everyone, when they see a herd, says "cows," not "cattle." Anyway, Rambles started along the trail following Jessie.

The trail began at an angle along the cliff and then wound its way down. To call it a "trail" is being generous. It was a spot where cows went down to get water, but not something any ranger in a national park would call a trail.

Below the top part of the trail was a big slab of slick rock that was tilted. Rambles saw the horses down below, and instead of following Jessie down, she decided to cut across the slick rock. The rock was tilted more than she figured. About halfway across the slab of rock, gravity took over, and she did a slow roll sideways off the rock, all four feet tipped up into the air, and she seemed to hang there like it was all in slow motion. Then she landed upside down in a scraggly cottonwood tree that was growing out of the side of the cliff.

LaVar's boy and I shimmied out as far as we dared across the slick rock and took a look. Both of us started cussing. I mean, what else was there to do? Those down below started cussing too. About six people, including Bob, LaVar, and Jessie, gathered below under the tree, looking up. I could see that one of Rambles' legs was caught between the cliff and a thick branch, and she was wedged in tight.

There was no way to get to her. During a lull in the cussing, Jack said, "Dammit, I didn't bring a gun this time." No one else had one either. None of us wanted to leave her there to suffer, and all of us were sure she would break a leg or something if we tried getting her out. Being upside down like that, she would suffocate before anything else happened to her. A horse's gut is too heavy for them to get enough air in their lungs if they're stuck upside down.

Eventually, we all stood there, staring at that young, pretty horse upside down in the tree, doomed. We'd run out of cuss words, even.

Rambles whinnied a couple of times. Then, when no one came to her rescue, she started to wriggle. I had scooted down on my butt far enough on the rock that I had a good view.

There was a loud *crack* like a gunshot, but it turned out to be the biggest branch breaking. Then *lots* of branches started to break, and Rambles began struggling in earnest. All of a sudden, the tree let her go. She rolled over in midair, headed straight down. The tree was about fifty feet up the side of that cliff.

The people under the cottonwood scattered, like roaches when the light goes on, and Rambles landed feet first in soft sand up to her knees.

None of us could believe it at first. Jessie spent a good five minutes looking her over, but the only casualty was the saddle. It was new and now had that broke-in look—scuffs and scratches everywhere.

Rambles came away from that with only one little scratch on her belly.

The rest of us led our horses down instead of turning them

loose, except Mom. She stayed in the saddle, and good old Tonto took her down the cliff face like he was walking down a country lane. No big deal.

SNAKE!

On the way to the Great Panel in Horseshoe Canyon, you have to ride down some slick rock and then turn a corner on a cliff face. They've put a gate there now, but when this story happened there was no gate, and that was a good thing. It's a trail going up the side of the cliff that's three to four feet wide. Most people these days walk in, but we always ride. We were on our way up the trail heading back to the trailers when Mom's mare, Sis, began to tightrope the very edge of the trail. The trail at that point is about 100 feet up the side of the cliff.

I hollered, "Mom, pull her over!"

It didn't matter what Mom did. That mare stayed on the edge for about ten feet before she would listen to Mom and go back to the middle. About that time Hotshot, who I was riding, walked over the top of the sidewinder rattlesnake that Mom's mare had seen but my colt hadn't. Hotshot was only three, but still, you'd think he'd see the snake. Luckily, he didn't step on it or get bitten. Maybe it was a good thing he didn't see the snake. He might have jumped off the cliff to get away from it instead of tight-roping the edge.

I hollered at Mom that there was a snake on the trail. Bob was riding point in front of Mom and heard me. He started yelling, "Get to the top NOW!"

Well, Mom and I didn't know what he was yelling for, but we hustled the horses into a trot until we reached the top. Bob ordered, "Jump off your horse and get your Mom's reins!"

Mom had time to start asking, "What?" when the gun went off.

Well, I had a time of it keeping ahold of Hotshot and Sis as the shot echoed around the canyon walls. Hotshot backed up almost to the edge, and they had my arms stretched out far enough my feet were almost off the ground because Mom's mare had jumped the opposite way.

It took a minute or so for the horses to settle down. Bob had known his uncle Doug, who was behind us, would shoot that snake if he saw it. He didn't want me and Mom to end up flying off the cliff on a spooked horse.

These days, the rattlesnakes are protected. They do serve an important function keeping the rat and mouse population down, but you'd have a hard time convincing those old cowboys of that.

AT THE TRACK

When we moved in with Bob, he was racing chariot and flat-track horses. He had a string of broodmares and would race the colts. As a horse-crazy teenager, I was in seventh heaven. Bob was an unusual cowboy in that he thought girls were as capable as boys. And he was crazy enough to let a green kid ride his racehorses. I was a know-it-all teenager, but I did listen to his advice most of the time. He taught me a lot about racing horses, and even more about how horses think.

Racing horses is fun, and most of the horses enjoy it as much as their riders do. They like to pit themselves against other horses and outrun them.

I was too tall as a teenager to be a jockey, but I was skinny enough to be an exercise rider. I spent a couple of summers galloping racehorses. The Golden Spike track in Brigham City had the best footing at that time, so most of the racehorse people took their horses there. It was perfect for me—Willard was only five miles from the track.

I learned a few more things, like how bad gnats taste when you're galloping along with your mouth open, and that killdeer birds like to dive-bomb people and horses. I found out that horses are exercised no matter what the weather is like, and that trainers prefer early mornings.

Some trainers don't train their racehorses very well; they figure the exercise rider can work out the kinks. After all, the colt only has to run in a big circle anyway.

Some horses have their own ideas, too, especially the smart

ones. There was one big chestnut Thoroughbred I galloped for a trainer that was smarter than average. He liked to win races, but he thought exercise was boring. He came up with his own brand of fun. Every so often, he'd get tired of galloping in the endless circle, so he'd turn and jump the rail and race to the trailer. Usually, I stayed on for the trip, but sometimes I'd hit the dirt when he did his about-face.

Like the stories about the Old Ranch, some stories connected with racehorses stand out more than others.

MUDDY TRACKS

I started a little brown mare for Vern, who was a friend of Bob's. He wanted to run the little filly on the track. The man was kind enough to take a chance on a girl trainer, which was unusual back then. I got her ready to run and used to the gates, then Vern took her from there. The little mare was quite talented and even went on to win a few races. She was small and dark brown with lots of muscle in all the right places. She had mutton withers like a lot of Quarter Horses do, especially the young ones. It was a challenge to keep a saddle on her.

We had worked her enough at the track that she was fairly well legged up (racehorse lingo for "in shape"). We had started gate schooling the little mare when another trainer asked if we would blow out the filly with his colt. "Blow out" means to start in the starting gates and run fast for a short distance, like in a real race.

The trainer's colt was the same age as the little brown mare, but at least five inches taller. The jockey grinned at me, and I saw the smirk on his face when we agreed to it. He was sure he would win the "race." One: I was a girl, and therefore an inferior rider, of course. And two: his horse would clearly have the advantage of a longer stride.

It had been pouring rain earlier and was still sprinkling, so the track was a muddy morass. Racehorses go out in all weather, and they need to learn to cope with it, so there was no question about putting the workout off for another day.

My uncle Richard happened to be visiting that day and had come out to watch us give the racehorses their workouts. Being a city guy, Richard had never seen horses work out in person. He and Mom took places at the colt finish line, and Bob went down to the gates to head the filly (that means to hold her head straight in the starting gate so she's looking down the track).

We trotted out past the stands and gave them a light gallop down to the gates. I was wishing I'd put the over-girth on the saddle—the track was as sloppy as I'd ever seen it. I put on three extra pairs of goggles just in case. You tie them in the back, and then you can whip the dirty one off and can see for a while until it's time to whip the next one off. A four-goggle track is a bad track.

We loaded the horses in the gates, and I grabbed a handful of her thick black mane.

Slam! The gates flew open, and the little filly launched forward. I felt the saddle slip back and was glad we had a breast collar on her to keep it from going too far. Then she was launching forward again, and I was amazed. We had never asked her to run against another horse before. She was *fast!* She was matching the big sorrel stride for stride, and we were nearing the colt finish line in nothing flat.

Right before we got there, I felt the saddle start to go sideways. I stomped in the near stirrup to right it, but it was no good. The saddle continued to slide over. We flashed by the colt finish line, and I had totally forgotten about the race since I was soon to lose my perch, and I *really* didn't want a mud bath. I kicked my feet free of the stirrups at the same moment that the saddle slipped all the way over and under her belly.

I waited for her to start bucking. Horses usually do when the saddle slips like that, especially green two-year-olds. The track was too muddy, and we were going way too fast to bail off. I grabbed ahold of her thick mane again and jerked myself back in the middle every couple of strides as we rounded the corner of the track.

Above the sound of her feet slapping the mud, I could hear Richard laughing. I was sure he was getting a grand show as he watched me try to keep my seat.

We rounded the curve, and I kept hollering "Whoa!" When she straightened out on the backside, I dared let go of her mane and pulled on the reins.

She began to slow down, and then I saw the sorrel colt pass us on the outside. His reins were flopping loose and his saddle was under his belly. There was no jockey in sight.

It turned out that when we passed the colt finish line and I started scrambling to keep my dry seat, the other horse's saddle had slipped sideways too. It went fast enough that the jockey was launched off to the side, and he landed with a splash right next to the rail at Richard's feet.

I pulled the little filly down to a trot and went over to catch the sorrel colt. He was tuckered out and felt lost without his rider, so he came on over to me and the filly. I rode the mare and ponied the colt over to where everyone was gathered at the colt finish line.

The jockey was soaked. Only his eyes and hair were free of mud, where the goggles and helmet had protected him.

Everyone but the jockey and I had tears in their eyes, they had laughed so hard.

YOU NEVER KNOW

A lot of cowboys don't like a girl doing "cowboy" things. Many tend to be chauvinistic when it comes to women. Luckily for me, Bob was not a chauvinist. When Mom married Bob, he was chariot racing with the Wasatch club. When he saw I was interested in driving the chariot horses, we started running at the Brigham track. Bob knew the Wasatch drivers would try to run a girl driver off the track. We had also recently moved to Willard, so the Brigham track was closer anyway. People are more tolerant now, but at that time, girls just didn't drive chariot horses. I was part of a very short list; there were three of us. When I was driving, it was the heyday of chariot racing, and it was the most popular it's ever been. The races went from noon until after four. Often, to get done before dark, we had to run three teams in each race.

This story is another I wrote when I was twenty and attending Weber State. We were supposed to write a true-life story about something from personal experience. When you live a certain way, it's easy to forget that other people can't relate to your life. The students in the class were supposed to critique our writing. When I got mine back, several said they liked the story but wondered if I realized "biographical writing" meant it was supposed to be a true story. Some of them had never heard of chariot racing. If you are one of those, look it up on Google and YouTube, and the following story will make more sense.

Modern chariot racing (as opposed to the Roman kind) was invented mostly so the racehorse guys would have something to do with their racehorses in the winter, and to keep the horses in shape year-round. It's done for fun, and believe me, most of the horses think it's as much fun as the people do.

"You never *know*," is a phrase racehorse people like to use. It means that no matter what has happened in the past, you can never be certain what will happen today.

***

I woke with my eyes wide open. My calico cat Tiki glared as I pushed her off the bed and swung my legs over the side. A queasy feeling washed over me. "You will not be nervous," the little voice inside my head said. I've always felt there are two of me: the me that people see, and a strangle little voice, calmer and more logical, that could be annoying because its predictions were so often right.

Bob was already at the arena to feed the racehorses their grain and take their water away. They get queasy too. I thought for a minute how lucky I was. Bob is my step-dad. When Mom married him, I was in heaven. Horses everywhere, and he was actually interested in showing me the "ropes." We became the best of friends, and Mom was truly happy. Sure, there are down times in everything, but they didn't count for much anymore.

I put on layer after layer of clothes and gritted my teeth when a blast of cold air bit my face as I opened the back door. My moon boots crunched on the frozen ground. When I got to the corral behind our house, the horses trailed after me, nickering every few steps to be sure I wouldn't forget I was there to feed them. "Geez, this is fun," I told myself sarcastically while I waited for the water buckets to fill up. I held my hand under my armpit to keep it warm and switched hands with every bucket, praying it would warm up before the races started so we wouldn't run on ice.

Back at the house, I stripped the top layers of clothes off and welcomed the warmth inside. Mom was bustling about the kitchen, creating various mouth-watering aromas as she cooked breakfast. I felt a slight pang of guilt because I wouldn't be able to eat much. My stomach would rebel at food on race days.

Bob had returned and sat forward in his old brown chair, a contrast to his usual casual slump. His beat-up gray cowboy hat was still on his head, almost the same color as his soft silver hair.

I sat down to watch cartoons and pretend it was just a normal day. Nobody wants to admit they're "racey," which means too nervous to remember your own name. It was a weekly joke to ask someone what their name was and laugh at the blank look on their face. You could laugh because you knew you'd do the same thing.

Right about then, Hal knocked on the door. "Come on in, Hal," Mom hollered, and our race partner walked in. Hal was a great partner. He was always there to help, always paid his way, and absorbed anything you could tell him about horses and racing. He didn't really love horses for themselves, but he did love racing, especially chariots. He was incredibly skinny, with jet-black hair and a face that looked better with a beard.

He stepped through the front room doorway, stared at the TV, and rolled his eyes. He knew it was pointless to say anything about the cartoons. Once, he had squealed on us and told everyone in the hanger at Hill that we watched cartoons on Saturday mornings, on race days, even! Only to start a discussion on which was the best. Bob's favorite, the Road Runner, won. Hal gave up ribbing Bob about watching kid cartoons.

Later, bone-chilling air met me as I opened the door to the arena. The humidity there always meant it would be about five degrees cooler than outside, and that day it was *cold*. The expanse of wood frame and steel walls loomed dimly. I turned up my collar to ward off some of the chill. Little puffs of dust floated up with each step I took. That place could spoil you in winter, even if it was cold. You could ride in dust clouds when the world outside was covered in ice and snow.

I rounded the turn past the hay and peered down the aisle. All the other horses were contentedly munching, but Buddy stuck his head out his stall window and looked at me as if to say, "Are we leaving yet?" I smiled at him and pulled his old blue halter off the wall.

Hal hurried in as I was grooming his horse, Zipper Bob. He hurried everywhere, and he paced as I worked on the horse, talking about the horses in quick little sentences. I concentrated on braiding the horse's mane. There is a point in braiding their tails.

Nobody wants a heavy, muddy tail wrapped around the lines. But braiding their manes is just for looks. Every time I did the manes, I asked myself why I'd freeze my fingers to put pom-poms on the horse. People do silly things.

"Well, I gotta pick up the kids," I announced as I finished. I was the racing club's secretary, and that meant getting to the races early and picking up the gate ticket girls. It was easier for me to have something besides horses to do on race days. Then I didn't get quite as nervous.

A little while later, I gazed out the window of the warm secretary's cubbyhole under the announcer's stand. Before me lay the wide muddy track, and two teams of horses were headed for the gates. They were all decked out in pom-poms and matching harness. The infield beyond looked barren compared to three weeks before. The massive crowd and myriad horse trailers were gone. Just the usual regulars remained. My mind wandered back to Shriner's Day, and I grinned.

***

Shriner's Day, the start of the chariot racing season, was the day you showed everyone what kind of team you had for the year. Everyone was there; all the chariot clubs from miles around. Even though the races on that day were a benefit to raise money for the Shriner's Hospital, not race points, it counted in friendships and fun.

In my mind, we were rounding the far turn and heading for the gates. Clyde drove the team on the way down so my hands wouldn't freeze. He was a tall, strong man. Unlike many big men, he was quiet with horses and people. His horses were always mellow. We were talking to the other drivers, using phrases like, "Ya ready for this?" and "What horse ya got there?" and "Track's pretty good!" "Pretty good" in chariot racing parlance meant you only needed two or three pairs of goggles.

Rex was driving up on my left with his team of sorrels, and Reese was on my right with a team of browns. Bob and Hal had cooked up the race against those guys. On Shriner's Day, you could

137

race who you wanted. None of them had asked me if *I* wanted to run in a three-team race. It was only my second year driving, and I had never been in the middle, so I was worried.

We bantered with each other until we passed the new cinderblock "Weenie Wagon" (refreshment stand) addition with its row of big windows. Our club had pitched in during the summer and built it. We were lucky we had. This was the biggest crowd ever, and the grounds were overflowing with people. They looked like multi-colored penguins in their coats and moon boots as they lined the white rail.

I heard my name from among the crowd amid shouts of "Get 'em, Ruth!" I couldn't often pick out individual faces because there were so many, but I could always spot Mom. Maybe moms send out vibes or something. There she was with a worried smile, pink cheeks, and earmuffs, perched on the small grandstand.

We passed the crowd, and the jingle of our gold and burgundy harness was suddenly loud. Buddy pranced and jigged, excited to get going, but Zipper would rather have walked to the gates. Clyde tapped Zipper with the whip a couple of times and said, "Zip, wake up!" to get him in the mood. I grabbed the whip, and he handed me the lines.

"You've got 'em," he said. "Keep a little to the right of your lane, don't worry about Rex. Reese is the one you'll have to beat today. Good luck!" Clyde always told it like it was and never gave you extras to worry about.

I pulled ahead of Rex to turn into the center gate and mumbled, "Good luck!" with the whip in my mouth. He mumbled the same back, and we were in the chutes to the gates. I looked up at Ralph in his rickety starter's box and knew I better be ready. He waited for horses to stand still, not drivers.

"Come around Zip, Buddy! Come around," I told them, and we swung into the gates. The headers reached down and pushed the horses' noses straight. Rex pulled into the right gate, and Reese waited on the left. I went over my checklist: good grip on the handle, whip just right, lines even with enough slack, knees bent. The little voice in my head said, "You're gonna do it!"

Haunches dropped in unison and the gates swung open: *Slam!*

Time became distorted. There was the expected jerk on my arm that held the handle as the horses surged forward. One stride—everything in slow motion, yet faster than you can think. All movement was subconscious, rehearsed.

"Yah!" we all shouted together.

Two strides—the walls flashed by. Three strides—sight and sound assailed me as we flew past the walls. Four strides—thirty-five miles an hour in forty-eight feet.

Dirt stung my face, and I saw Reese's team out of the corner of my eye. They were even with our chariot.

"Yah!" I sounded like a banshee.

Moving all in one piece, we drifted a little to the right. "Come on, Zip! Come on, Buddy!" Speech had returned.

Reese pulled up on us, and there was no sign of Rex. Suddenly, the sound of the crowd rushed up like breakers in the sea. Colors flashed by. We flew past the colt finish line. One hundred yards to go, and brown horses loomed large at our side. Then Buddy and Zip turned on the afterburners. The roar of the main crowd was deafening. We passed the finish line two lengths ahead!

"Way to go, boys!" I screamed.

Our Shriner's Day win. Bob invited Rees to be in the picture with us.

***

"Ruth!" Mom's voice brought me back to the present day.

"Ruth, you had better go get hooked up."

I squinted at the winter sun as I crossed the track and pondered our chances. I hiked over the banks of snow that had been pushed aside to make roads for the horse trailers. We had won all our races up to that point. But since winners draw against winners, you never know.

Bob and Hal had already unloaded the team and pulled their blankets off. They looked funny with their slick bodies and fuzzy necks.

Buddy was an average-sized gelding with a deep sorrel coat, four stocking legs, and a big bald face. He was a classy-looking horse.

Zipper was a strange horse to be around. He was casual about life. One day was just as good as the next for him. He liked to race, and that was a good thing. His was the kind of personality that would not have run if he didn't want to. Zip was a tall, long bay horse with a lot of muscle. When we started running him, we had to add a foot to our chariot tongue.

We jingled down the track, and Clyde said, "They feel the best they've felt all year, you'll get 'em." He stepped off the chariot right before we pulled into the gates.

I was in the same gate I had been in on Shriner's Day, except this time it was only a two-team race. I gripped the handle and noticed my lines were twisted. I wondered if I should fix them. Then the little voice in my head calmly said, "It doesn't matter, you won't finish anyway." I had a second to think to myself, "What a crazy thing to say."

I could hear Grant's team moving around in their gate. Buddy started to back up. *Slam!* The gates swung open, and Zipper Bob launched forward. There were almost no horses in our part of the country that could start as fast as Zipper, but Buddy could. Not that day, though.

Buddy couldn't start because he got nervous and began to back up, so when Zipper took off, he scooped Buddy up and the chariot, too. I was suddenly looking at Buddy's broad back. The metal chariot hub made a horrid scraping sound on the plywood, and splinters flew. I grabbed the other side of the chariot so I wouldn't slam into the wall. The chariot lurched over onto its side.

Buddy was on his feet and running then. At once, I was sliding on my stomach like a kid on a toboggan. I could hear the gate crew yelling, "Let go of the lines!" I looked at my outstretched hand as I slid faster, but my hand was empty. I had landed on the line, and it was pulling the horses into the rail. The end slapped my face as it was pulled free, and I yelled, "Whoa!" Not that the horses could have heard me or listened to the command if they could. Visions of horses' legs meeting metal rail zoomed through my mind.

Zipper saved the day. He was almost lying sideways, trying not to hit the rail. It grazed his side and even took a strip of hair off. Then they straightened up and went clattering down the track.

Bob was suddenly at my side. He sure could move fast when his kid was lying on the track. Maybe we should have hooked him up with Zipper instead of Buddy.

"Stupid horse didn't start," I complained as the gate crew flocked around. My voice sounded funny, and I realized my teeth were still clenched on the whip. The gate crew could see I was alright, so we all turned to find out what had become of the team. Good old Zipper ran the race like normal and was slowing down on the backside. After all, it was simply another day for him.

At the horse trailer, as we cooled the horses off, I watched Buddy walk in slow, painful circles and wondered if it was worth it to make them run. Then the crash of the gates was heard in the distance, and the clatter of the chariots, shouting of the drivers, and the thunder of racing horses could be heard. Buddy swung his head around, flipped his tail over his back, and pranced around like a colt. His eyes sparkled, and he watched the teams all the way past the finish line.

The two of me said as one, "We don't make them run, they run because they love it."

The track photographer caught photos of our wreck.

HERE, HOLD THIS

Bob was always thinking up ways to add humor to life from his perspective. Other people were a handy thing to target.

Racehorses are walked around in circles after they race so their muscles don't cramp up, especially when it's winter. It's called cooling out and is not a very exciting job. Bob was an expert at pawning his horse off on someone else.

He'd walk casually over to some unsuspecting person and begin a conversation. Shortly into their talk, he would pretend he needed something out of his pockets—something that required two hands. He'd say, "Here, hold this," and hand them the horse's lead rope. Then the other person would end up with a horse to cool out. Most would fall for his tricks more than once. And many were good-humored about it and would cool out the horse for him.

One person that fell for it nearly every time was his friend Danny. He ended up cooling out Bob's horse quite frequently. It was a gamble to pawn a horse off on Danny, though. When someone would wave at Danny, he often had a cigarette or beer can in his free hand, so he'd let go of the hand holding the horse and wave back. Hal pointed out to Bob that when you pawn a horse off on someone else to do your work, you can't complain about how they go about it.

One day, Danny paid Bob back in spades, although Danny didn't do it on purpose.

It had snowed a *lot* that week. Enough that they had to plow lanes in the snow so we could pull our trailers into the infield. We were getting set up for the races and had barely unloaded the horses when Bob noticed the trailer was leaking inside. There was about a half foot of snow on top. It was heavy enough it hadn't blown off when we drove over.

Bob asked Danny if he'd help pull the snow off the top. They both climbed up on the tire wells, then hooked their boot toes into the slats on the side so they could start at the front of the trailer. Bob tossed a lead rope over to Danny. They clung to the side of the trailer with one hand and started pulling the snow over the side by sliding the lead rope back and forth.

As you can imagine, it wasn't a very good perch. Hal was standing next to me, and he handed me his horse's lead rope, saying, "Here, hold this." I scowled at him but took the horse, and he gave me a wicked grin.

I soon found it wasn't tricking me that he was grinning about. I was standing at the front of the truck so I could see both sides. I wanted to see who got the most snow on them as they tried Bob's innovative snow removal idea.

Hal walked casually past the truck, and when he got near where Danny was perched on the trailer, he said, "Hi, Danny," and waved. Danny always returned a wave. Since one hand was occupied with holding him onto the side of the trailer, he let go of the lead rope to wave back at Hal.

Bob couldn't recover when the lead rope suddenly went slack. He was only holding onto the side of that trailer by his toes and fingertips, anyway. He fell backwards, arms flailing, and landed with a *poof* in the fluffy snow beside the trailer. The snow settled back down, and Bob was covered in it from head to toe.

They decided to leave the snow on the trailer. Danny swore he would not let go again and would help him finish cleaning it off, but Bob didn't take him up on that.

IT'S WHAT'S INSIDE
THAT COUNTS

When I was eighteen, the horse trainer I was working for moved out of the stable he was renting. I took a gamble and decided to rent it myself. We called the place simply the Arena, although officially on my paperwork it was Wrench Cross Stables. I trained and boarded out of there for six years. There were thirty-three stalls in the place, so I would sublet part of them to another trainer. The first one was a racehorse trainer. At the time, he was the top trainer of Quarter Horses in the Intermountain area. I learned a lot from him about racing horses.

Sometimes, the stars align and a horse is lucky enough to end up doing what they love to do and excels at it. Rocket Launcher was one, and Happy Go Lucky was another. That year, Rocket Launcher was the world champion chariot horse. The buddy horse he ran with was no slouch either, but everyone knew Rocket was the fastest.

The trainer had to go out of town on weekends fairly regularly to take horses to the races. He started trusting me enough to take care of things when he was away. Rocket had to be kept in shape more than most horses because if he wasn't, his legs, which were already trashed from years of racing, would not be salvageable. His front legs always had to be kept wrapped, so he was high maintenance but good to be around.

Rocket would get sore legs if he was ridden, so I'd wrap his legs and pony him ("pony" means lead another horse while you're riding) on the soft track the trainer had made along the rail of the outdoor arenas that were farther up the hill, east of the indoor arena. When you pony a horse, they're supposed to stay behind the lead horse (the one you're riding), but Rocket would fuss and balk and generally be a pain—unless you let him get his nose out front, then he'd gallop along, happy as a clam. He *loved* to win.

Besides learning how to wrap legs and keep a horse sound enough to run, I also learned consistency from watching the trainer. He kept his barn neat and orderly and had a specific schedule tailored to each individual horse. There were many reasons he was the top trainer. Another was that he understood how horses think. Like Bob, he knew how to get the horses to *want* to do what he asked them, rather than *making* them do it.

The arena was only about a hundred feet from a fairly busy highway. Any farmer will tell you that critters get loose sometimes. It's inevitable. Those racehorses were worth tens of thousands of dollars. When one of the trainer's horses would get loose and run around pell-mell, he would yell at anyone who started running or shouting to calm down and move slow. Most people tend to get too excited and start yelling and trying to contain the horse, which usually backfires and spooks the loose horse more. But the trainer would go get a can of grain, casually walk over near the escapee, and shake that can of grain. The horse would come to investigate, and he'd turn and walk back to the arena. Presto, the horse is caught! I've used that technique countless times since, and it always works—*if* no one gets the horses too excited first.

I learned another quite unexpected lesson from that trainer.

There were rumors floating around the racehorse community that he was gay. Shortly after he moved into the arena, I met his girlfriend. She insisted she knew for a fact he wasn't, and that I better not step in on her. Once she figured out that I didn't intend to be competition in that way, she was okay and turned out to be a nice person.

About six months after he started training out of the arena, it was late evening, and I was heading home. It wasn't unusual for him and one or two of the hands (in horse-speak, a "hand" is an assistant who is good at their job) who worked for him to still be there. I said goodbye and went home. I had only been in the house a few minutes when I realized I had forgotten something (I don't recall what) at the arena, so I went back.

The arena had a foyer lined with pictures of various races the trainer's horses had won. There was a small office in one corner, and an old green couch sat outside the office against the north wall. They must not have heard me drive up because when I came through the door, the trainer and the jockey were quite involved with each other. They weren't naked, but they were getting there, hands and lips traveling everywhere. Not knowing what to do, I just said "hi" and kept on going into the arena. I could feel my face burning from embarrassment as I walked across the arena and over to my part of the barn.

The trainer caught up with me when I was coming back out of my tack room with whatever it was I had come back for. I stared at his boots at first, not wanting to look him in the face. I didn't know if he would be angry, or embarrassed like I was. He stood there and didn't say anything, so I screwed up the courage to look him in the face.

I was relieved to see he was embarrassed and not angry. He was also worried, but I didn't catch on to that at first. He started to stammer something but stopped, stuck, not really knowing what to say.

We stared at each other for a moment, then I said, "It's not my business what you do or who you're with." We talked briefly then. I don't remember any other words specifically in that short conversation, but it dawned on me that he was very much afraid I would tell what I'd seen. I left shortly after.

He had always been a little standoffish before then, but when a little time went by and I didn't mention what I had seen to anyone, not even him, he was friendlier and we got along well.

He died of AIDS a few short years later. He was a good man and a great horse trainer, but if it were known he was gay, and not only suspected, he would not have been able to make a living doing what he loved as much as Rocket: racing. And winning.

What I learned was he did not choose to be like he was, he was simply wired that way. I suspected that was the case when I knew him, but Happy Go Lucky clinched that fact in my mind.

147

A couple of years later, the racehorse trainer moved on and another trainer rented some of the stalls from me. Vaughn was a show horse trainer, and he also excelled at his job. He and I had attended a Ray Hunt clinic the fall before and learned a better way to train horses—using the horse's basic nature to train them rather than endless repetition and force.

Vaughn was brought a stallion to train that was flat-out dangerous. The horse's name was Happy Go Lucky. The people who owned him had taken him to a couple of other trainers and he was broke to ride, but it was hazardous to be around him. He thought chasing people and taking a chunk out of them was fun. If he had been less valuable or less talented, he would have been gelded, or simply destroyed.

People make honest mistakes sometimes, and Happy Go Lucky's problem was one. When he was a little colt, they had thought it was fun to let him chase them out of the corral, and then when he grew to weigh in at around 1,400 pounds, they didn't know how to fix it.

The horse had no ground manners. Not a good thing for a stallion. When he arrived, Vaughn asked Irv the horse shoer (no one in our part of the country calls them farriers) and me to stand on the outside of the round corral and get him out if the horse got him down. Then he spent a couple of hours using two lariats—one on Happy's head and one on his flank—to stop him when he charged. Luckily, Happy wasn't very smart or innately mean. Some horses are, you know. Just like people.

Within a week, Happy was convinced Vaughn was God. Vaughn could take a bridle rein and loop it on Happy's front leg, and the stallion would lie down, totally relaxed. After that, anytime Happy would start acting aggressively, Vaughn would lay him down and pet him. The horse went on to qualify for the World Paint Show that year. Besides being talented, he did so well because he did not resist Vaughn. There was no tension in him, and it showed in the ring. The colt was one of those who knew when he was in the spotlight, and he would give a little extra when he was.

The next spring, the owners wanted to start breeding him. They had turned him out with mares when he was three but didn't get any colts, so they wanted Vaughn to hand-breed him (what that means is the stallion and mare are in halters, and handlers lead them to make sure the mare gets bred safely—safe for the horses, not the handlers).

Well, Happy wouldn't do it. Vaughn thought maybe the horse was so convinced Vaughn was the boss that he needed to stay away and let me or Irv be the handlers. Happy would nicker and nibble at the mare's flanks and generally do what stallions usually do to woo mares, but he wouldn't breed them.

Frustrated, Vaughn picked a mare who was more than willing to let the horse breed her and turned Happy loose in a round corral with her. Again, he would flirt but not actually do anything. He was four that year. Vaughn and the owners had him checked by a vet, and there was nothing wrong physically. They decided to give up on the breeding idea and show him one more year, then try the next spring.

About a week after they made that decision, Vaughn was riding Happy in the outdoor arenas. There were some pens alongside the north fence with horses in them. The Arena was overflowing with mares and foals in pens because it was spring. The mares were there to be bred for the next round of colts. Vaughn had five stud horses in training, and I had two.

Irv and I were riding in the indoor arena, and Vaughn came to get us. He had an idea. Vaughn had been riding Happy past the corrals, and every time they passed a certain gelding, Happy would get very excited—studhorse excited.

We took out the mare we wanted Happy to breed with. Then Vaughn brought out the gelding. We led Happy over to the two horses. He was clearly more excited about the gelding. The gelding got a little wild-eyed and danced around, but all that did was get Happy more excited.

We waited until he was ready, then we put him on the mare. We got Happy to breed three mares that spring by teasing him with the gelding he was in love with.

That's not the funniest part.

In the fall of his fifth year—his third trip to the World Paint Show—Happy was bought by some people from Germany. The next spring, Vaughn got a call. They knew Happy had sired some foals, but they couldn't get him to breed any mares. They also wanted Vaughn to show them the cues (signals from horse to rider) he used for riding and showing, so they paid for him to fly over and stay for a week.

Irv and I couldn't wait for him to come back. We had to find out how you translate "your horse is gay" into German. Vaughn said when he got there, he took Happy on a tour of their barn and corrals until he found a gelding Happy was attracted to. Then he had the translator explain. I asked if they were angry. He said that once the light went on in their minds and they realized they had bought a gay horse, they laughed so much their sides hurt.

For safety reasons, most stallions are taught to use a dummy for breeding, and it wasn't long before Happy caught on to that.

The thing is, I'm sure horses don't choose to be gay. Some people might, but I'm betting most don't; it's simply how they were born.

I didn't take many photos when I was at the arena. I was too busy. But I do have these of Happy. He was a slob, and he was mostly white, so it was quite a chore to get him clean for a show and keep him that way. Vaughn used Tide to wash the green off the horses. It was cheap and worked well. I was often enlisted to help out. One day, we took these pictures when we were giving Happy a bath—our own little Tide commercial.

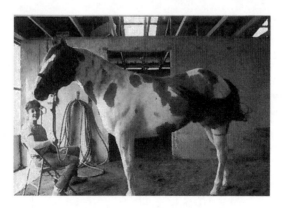

BUDDY

I got a horse instead of a car for my sixteenth birthday. The best birthday present *ever!* He was the horse I tried everything on first, and he was game to give things a shot no matter what I asked.

Buddy's build was almost a mirror image of the famous painting of a Quarter Horse that Tom Mix painted, except Buddy had four stocking legs, a flax mane and tail, and a bald face. There are a couple of idioms in the racehorse industry. One is that if they're too good looking, they won't run well, and the other is that the more white they have, the slower they run. The second one is actually true, statistically speaking, for some odd reason. The first one—well, when Buddy was two, there were only two horses in the whole Intermountain area who could even come close to outrunning him on a good day.

Buddy was the first colt I started (trained), along with his chariot buddy BJ. Buddy would always try his best and wanted to please. BJ would always argue first. I learned what things should feel like when they're right from Buddy. I learned how to win arguments from BJ.

Bob was offered a lot of money for Buddy. Even though he was a gelding, the racehorse guys knew a good one when they saw one, but Bob gave him to me. I put a lot of miles on Buddy. His job, when he wasn't running himself, was to pony the other horses. I was also taking lessons on how to ride in shows and rodeo queen contests. Then I got into reining and showing at the Quarter Horse shows, and Buddy was game to try it all. We even drove him in downtown Ogden pulling carriages one summer.

Bob would not have been able to afford a horse with Buddy's breeding, normally. But Buddy's owner had passed away, and the widow did not know what to do with a pasture full of horses. When Bob bought him, the colt was a yearling and starving. He had a parrot mouth (which means he had a bad overbite), and the grass in the pasture he'd been living in was too short for him to get enough to eat. A horse with a parrot mouth has to tear the grass off instead of bite it.

He was a pitiful sight when Bob brought him home. Mom and Bob were newlyweds and we had just moved in with Bob in his place in Clinton. Buddy had a big pot belly from worms and malnutrition, and he was missing some hair, too. It wasn't long before his deep sorrel coat gleamed, and Buddy *loved* Bob. He would follow him wherever he went. Bob called him a "pocket" horse since he was always in your back pocket.

Later, when I began showing horses instead of racing, Bob had to hide where Buddy couldn't see him, or all the horse would do was look at Bob instead of paying attention to what he was supposed to do.

Buddy was the horse I learned on first for practically everything, and galloping horses as an exercise rider was one of the first things. At that time, we would go out to Bob's friend's place who had a dirt track cut out of his cornfield. It was a small track, about a quarter mile all the way around. I was galloping Buddy, and there was a big bang. I never did find out what it was, but Buddy spooked and took off, and I had my first taste of what it's like riding a runaway.

Luckily, Buddy stayed on the track. I lost my stirrups, but I was a lot more agile then and stayed on. I tell you what—that horse was *fast!* When we went whizzing by, Bob hollered, "Just keep him on the track, you can ride as fast as he can go!" He was right, as usual.

When Buddy got tired and wanted to stop, Bob had me run him some more, which is the cure for a horse that runs away. When we were done and Buddy and I were dripping wet and panting from our efforts, Bob explained why he'd made me keep the horse going. After that, Buddy never did run away again.

One of Buddy's flat-track win pictures.

GOOD NEIGHBORS

There's something special about small towns. Not long ago, our little Aussie dog, Charlie, got scared and ran off when the butcher came to get the pigs. My husband called a couple of friends, and soon almost a dozen people dropped what they were doing, even two of the city cops, and were out searching for one mutt. Yep, small towns and the people in them are special.

Another time, people appeared out of the woodwork to rescue old Buddy. He was nearing thirty that winter. A lot of people in town knew him, and many in the county. There hadn't been a horse in the county who could outrun him when he was two.

Buddy was also the lesson horse for countless kids, so he was sort of a celebrity in the area and had earned his retirement.

There is a pond fed by a spring across the gravel drive from our house. I had a couple of the horses out there in the pond pasture for the winter. As I stepped out of the garage door, I remember noticing Buddy standing on the ice on top of the pond and thinking, "That's a stupid place to stand" before going on to feed the pasture horses.

There was no one around at that moment. I started feeding and headed for the pond last. No Buddy could be seen. Heart sinking, I ran through the gate, and sure enough, he had fallen through the ice. I shouted for Jennifer, my daughter, who was coming out of the house, to go get Robert. Then I booked it to the barn and got a halter and some ropes.

The ice was about five inches thick where he'd fallen through, and his legs were sunk into the mud. Luckily, he had not fallen through the deeper end. But he could not get a purchase on the muddy bottom to jump out of there.

Robert got the sledgehammer with the thought that he could break a path for the horse. It was below freezing that evening, and the horse was not going to last long. The only thing out of the icy water was his shoulders, neck, and head. We pulled and encouraged him to jump out, but there was no way he could have.

Suddenly, people came from everywhere. Sabrina and her mom, who boarded horses at my place, came over with ropes and a rug to maybe give him purchase for his front legs. Bob appeared with another sledgehammer, and Sean was suddenly there. His dad had run chariots with us when we were both kids and had helped us run Buddy on the flat track (racing with a rider in the saddle, as opposed to chariots). I have no idea how he knew something was wrong. He had never been to our place before. His mom's property bordered ours on the north.

The three men started taking turns with the sledgehammers, but it was a hopeless cause. The ice was too thick, and he'd gone down too far from the shore. Our tractor would not make it near enough to the pond. There were piles of snow in the way, and the horse was too heavy for us puny humans to pull out. It would not be long before he froze to death. It was getting dark, and we literally only had minutes remaining to save him.

Then Fred, our neighbor who owns a dairy, came over with his new four-wheel-drive tractor. It was all ice and steep down into the pond area. We cut the fence, and Fred's tractor was able to crawl over the snowbanks to get near the pond. We tried to get a strap around Buddy's chest for him to pull with, but it just wasn't possible. Fred told us he could pull the horse out, but he couldn't guarantee it wouldn't hurt him. Fred hooked a chain to the lead ropes on Buddy's halter and, running that tractor and bucket like a master musician, he carefully pulled Buddy out of the pond and never once jerked on the horse's head.

Buddy's legs were frozen. He couldn't tell where they were, but he scrambled onto his feet, and we threw blankets onto him. Then the question was how to get him dry. The temperature was near zero that evening.

Clay and Joe Thorpe, other neighbors who had appeared out of nowhere, thought up the solution. We cleared a spot in our garage for Buddy, and Robert got our shop vac. Clay brought down a space heater from his place, and voila—instant horse dryer. Buddy staggered to the garage, stubbing his toes on the slanted driveway. He clearly could not feel his feet.

Buddy had some small cuts on his legs from the sharp ice when he fell through. As they thawed out, the blood would start to flow. He only had those few cuts to show for his adventure. Buddy wasn't so sure about standing there in that strange garage with the loud blow-dryer. It was a little weird and scary, but he was too tired and cold to make a fuss.

Buddy didn't even catch cold. The story made the *Box Elder News* that week. They called me a couple of days after the incident to get the details. Yep, small towns and the people in them are special.

HOLY SMOKE!

Another idiom among horse people is, "If you ride, you're going to fall off." It really is inevitable. The first horse I was ever bucked off of was Cutty Sark. We hadn't been living with Bob for very long when he was crazy enough to let me exercise his two racehorses, Cutty and Holy Smoke. They were full sisters. Cutty was two and looked like her sire, with a dark-brown coat, lots of muscle, but not a lot of leg. Holy Smoke was a twin of her mother, Katy Adams—tall, lean, and bay. She was three.

I was very green as a rider and knew practically nothing, but I was game to try it out and lived for any moment I could get in the saddle. Galloping horses is pretty simple—trot and gallop in giant ovals—so I guess Bob figured I couldn't do too much damage, even as green as I was.

Did you know they use miniature horses as seeing-eye "dogs"? They're for people who are allergic to dog dander. Horses do not think like people do; they think like horses. But that doesn't mean they are stupid. There are also all kinds of levels of smart and dumb in horses, just like in people. Holy Smoke was on the smart side. If she had been small, she would have made a good seeing-eye horse herself.

As I mentioned, I was just learning to ride, and Bob was crazy enough to let me gallop his racehorses. For Holy Smoke, racing was fun, but exercising was *boring*. She liked to play with her rider just to add some spice to her day.

Bob had me ride Cutty for a few weeks before he put me on Holy Smoke. Then he had me gallop her. She bucked me off almost every day. If a simple crow hop didn't work, she'd duck one way or the other until I came off. Then, to add insult to injury, she'd run around for a bit, then come on over and stand by me, waiting for me to get back on so she could have some more fun.

After the first few rides, Bob left me to it. He knew Holy Smoke wasn't really mean, she was just playing, and I was young enough that the ground wasn't as hard as it is when you're older. I galloped them in the big pasture behind Bob's property. It was at least ten acres, and there were small cement ditches crossing it for irrigation water.

Holy Smoke saw those ditches as a good opportunity to goof off. Sometimes, she would spook at them when we got there and jump sideways; sometimes, she would leap over like they were the Grand Canyon. Other times, she would slide to a stop and snort at them like she'd never seen something so scary.

We were heading for one of those ditches, and I could feel her bunch up. I knew she was going to try bucking at the ditch, or maybe a slide stop. She took a leap over and kept on leaping into big crow hops. I resolved she wasn't going to dump me that time, so I clung on even when I went sideways and lost one stirrup. I pushed myself back up on her back with the one foot left in the stirrup.

I didn't know my foot was twisted backwards. I sprained my ankle badly. Pain shot through all of me. It was the first time I'd really been hurt when riding. I gritted my teeth as tears sprang up in my eyes. I was left gasping for breath and wondering how in the heck I was going to get back home. We were at the far end of the pasture, and there was no way I could walk. The only cell phones that existed then were those giant brick ones. Needless to say, I didn't have one.

I looked around, and no one was in sight. I knew that crazy filly would not let me hang onto her side and use her as a crutch. I figured she would just as soon dump me off and go home on her own.

When I gasped in pain, Holy Smoke stopped so that I didn't fall off. She stood stock-still while I assessed my situation and looked around for help. There was not a human soul in sight. Having no better options, I turned her toward home and hoped she would at least take me a little way before leaving me behind.

When we came to the ditch, she stepped across, delicate-like, and continued on. She did that with the next two ditches, and then we came to the gate between our place and the big pasture. She had never been taught to let a rider open a gate from the saddle, but that day she stood quietly, sideways to the gate, so I could reach down and open it. Then she waited for me to close it after we went through.

When one of the colts in our pasture came up to see us, she pinned her ears to warn him off and kept walking real slow and careful, like she was a good broke horse and I was a little toddler she was taking for a ride.

When we got to the barn, she let me open and close yet another gate from the saddle and stood quietly while I slid off. I pulled her bridle and saddle off, hanging onto her mane, and turned her loose in the barnyard, then I hopped to the house.

You'll hear people say horses are dumb. They do crazy things sometimes, that's for sure, but they're more aware of important things than we give them credit for.

RIGHT TURN

Mules are interesting creatures. They tend to take after the donkey side of their genetics rather than the horse. Donkeys evolved in mountainous regions where running away was often not an option. Therefore, they will usually stand and fight. A horse, being a creature from the wide-open steppes, would prefer to run away. And since a mule is a hybrid of the two equines, they are most often hardier and more intelligent than a horse. It is said that you must treat a mule like you should treat a horse, and for the most part, that is true. They don't take kindly to bad handling, and they will make you pay in all sorts of exotic ways if they are mistreated— or just because they think their ideas are better than yours, even if they aren't mistreated.

When we were racing flat-track horses, mule races were popular as well (flat-track is horse lingo for a normal horse race with a jockey in the saddle, as opposed to chariot racing). It was a good chance to see some fun since mules are not afraid to let anyone know their opinion of things.

We were at the track in Pocatello one Saturday when I was a teenager, and the race card had mule races mixed in. Buddy was two years old and had won his race that day, so we were in high spirits. His race had been at the beginning. We were hanging around waiting for the other horse our friend Ken was running. His gelding was in the next-to-last race. In the middle were the mule races.

We went down to the paddock to look them over and watch the fun. The paddock is where the public can get a good look at the prospects running in the race and decide which ones they want to bet on. We picked out our favorite for the race. Practically every mule in the race was a big brown, but I liked the looks of number three and placed a $2 bet on him. Truth be told, it was actually the looks of Shane, the jockey, that I liked. He was a better than average jockey, and certainly easier than average on the eye. We ran up to the stands to watch the race and see how our bets would pan out.

It took a while to load them in the gates, mules being mules, but eventually all of them were in the starting gate, and the starter pulled the lever to open them up. It was a good start. No one interfered with their neighbor, and the jockeys and the people in the stands started whooping and hollering to urge their mule on. It was only a quarter-mile race, so they were running flat-out from the start.

I don't know if it's still there, but at the Pocatello track, there was a small opening on the outside rail that led to the stalls on that side of the track. It was on the straightaway about halfway between the starting gates and the quarter-mile finish line. After about a hundred yards into the race, the mule on the inside rail started to pull away, and the cheering and shouting got louder, mine included. The first three numbers in the race were also the top three runners so far. The mule I bet on was running at the second mule's hip, and the three of them were widening the gap between the rest of the pack.

Without warning, the number two mule decided the barn looked more inviting than the finish line and did an abrupt right turn, heading for the hole in the fence. His jockey was suddenly left with only air under his breeches. And since the mule I bet on was on the tail of that mule, Shane went flying too. Both jockeys did a graceful somersault and came down feet first.

The other mules decided that was a great idea and followed the number two mule, and so it went all across the track. Jockeys and bat whips were tossed in all directions, limbs and legs helter-skelter, and they each landed with a puff of dust on the sandy track.

Every mule in the race except the one in the number one hole followed their buddy back to the barns. A couple of them missed the gap in the fence and had to spin a quick circle then dash out the hole. Shouting and cursing could be heard coming from the track as the jockeys picked themselves up, found their bat whips, and dusted off their breeches. The only injuries in that wreck were to their pride.

Once the jockeys all started moving and everyone could see they weren't hurt, the cursing was drowned out by the laughter from the crowd. It was awhile before I could catch my breath to speak, and my sides hurt clear past lunch that day from laughing so hard.

The only mule that finished the race was number one since he was on the inside and didn't see that his race buddies had a better idea than running a race.

We thought that was the best entertainment we were going to get that day. But once the loose mules were rounded up from wandering the barns, the next mule race on the ticket was brought to the paddock. Once again, we went down to pick out who we wanted to bet on and to watch the fun if any mules refused to move once they were saddled. Mules and donkeys really do that; sometimes Hollywood does get things right. It was entertaining seeing the jockeys and trainers persuade the ornery critters to move, and sometimes when they do start moving, they start bucking. Horses can be hard to handle in the paddock, too, but not usually as often or as spectacularly as mules.

In that race, there was a clear favorite. The black mule was big and unusually broad in the chest for a mule. He'd run six races so far that season and won them all by more than a length, which is no small feat in a quarter-mile race. The betting was light on the others in the field. Everyone was sure he would win again, so they put their money on him. I placed a $2 bet on a chestnut mule just because he was pretty (Shane wasn't in that race) and went up to the stand to watch the results.

As usual, it took a while to get the mules in the gate. I had never seen the black mule run before, but I could hear the crowd around me extolling his virtues and how awesome he was as a race mule. I heard them also saying he was unusually easy to handle for a mule. He'd drawn the number five hole in the gate, so we had a good view of him when the gates opened. It was an eight-mule race. The gates slammed open, and a wave of cheering rose up from the grandstands to match the pounding of the mules pelting down the track and the screams of encouragement from the jockeys.

After a few seconds, the dust down by the starting line cleared, and we could all see the number five mule's big broad chest framed in the starting gate. He hadn't moved at all. His jockey could be seen bouncing up and down to encourage him to go, and the starters were slapping him on the rump, but he wouldn't move.

There was a pause in the noise from the crowd when everyone realized the favorite was not in the race. I'm not sure anyone noticed who won, because about the time the rest of the runners dashed past the finish line, the big black mule started to bray.

A mule's bray is *very* loud. It carried down the track and could be heard even over the pounding of hooves. The majority of the crowd shouted their own versions of curse words, some of them not printable, and tossed their betting stubs down in disgust. The rest of us couldn't stop laughing.

It was a while before they could get the black mule to stop braying and take a step. I don't even remember where the chestnut I'd bet on placed, but I can still see that black mule standing in the gates while the others raced down the track as plain as day.

BORN ON THE FOURTH OF JULY

Clyde's story begins with a lightning storm in the early part of September. I was boarding a little brown Quarter Horse mare named Swifty for Stacy, a girl who took riding lessons from me. The field we pastured the horses in belonged to my brother. It was a long, narrow strip of open land about a quarter mile from one end to the other. A lightning storm had raged all night, and I hurried over to the pasture as soon as I ate breakfast to check on the horses. I had a feeling things weren't right. When I got there, I could see no horses in the field. I called Bob for help and gathered up all the halters I could find and a bucket of grain, thinking I would have to go find them and lead them home.

When I got back to the field, I started walking the fence. It wasn't long before I found them. They had broken the fence at the west end where Del kept his horses, and they were mixed in with them. It was quite an assortment of horses. Poor old Buddy, being the fastest among our horses, had hit the barbed wire fence first, and the skin on his face was literally hanging off his nose. He had a wide, bald face, and almost all of the white skin had been stripped in a big upside-down V starting between his eyes and on down to just above his nose. We called the vet and then started fixing fence and sorting horses while we waited.

There was a big bay draft looking colt with high stockings and a blaze face that kept getting in our way. I hadn't noticed him in Del's field before. He was very friendly and appeared to be a yearling, although he was as tall as any of the horses out there. Bob took a better look at him and said, "I think that's a horse colt," which in our part of the country means a colt that has not been gelded yet.

It was Acey the vet who came to stitch Buddy's face. We were all standing around and commenting on how horses look behind them to check they're ahead of the group instead of looking where they're going so they end up running into things. It was taking quite a while to sew Buddy up. By that time, Del was there, and Stacy was, too.

When Acey finished, he looked around at the horses and said, "Is that a horse colt?" Del assured us the guy he had just bought the colt from told him he'd gelded the colt. The colt was half Shire and half Clydesdale, and Del wanted to use him for pulling his wagons.

Stacy's horse Swifty and all the other horses looked no worse for wear. Buddy was the only casualty of the night. Eventually, Buddy's face healed up without a mark, except that he was missing half his forelock after that, and we settled in for the winter. As the days wore on, Swifty started gaining weight, which looked good on her at first since she had been on the slim side before that. Around February, I started to suspect there was more to this weight gain than fat. Stacy had ambitions to show Swifty at the Quarter Horse shows, and they were well on their way. Both she and the horse had talent. I was beginning to think Stacy was going to have to delay her showing days. In March, I decided I'd have to discuss this with her. When she next commented on Swifty's weight gain . . .

"Do you remember when they ran through the fence and poor old Buddy cut his face?" I said.

"Yes," she said.

"Remember that colt that kept getting in the way?" I asked.

"Yes," she replied.

I said, "I don't think that's fat."

She stood there for a moment, looking blank. Then the light went on. "That guy said the colt was a gelding!"

"Yep, but I think Swifty is going to have a colt. I'll call Del and check with him."

It took a couple of days to reach Del on the phone, which gave Stacy time to mull the news over. The call to Del went something like this:

"Hey, Del, how are things?" I asked.

"Fine, what's up?"

"You remember last September when the horses ran through the fence?"

"Oh yeah, that was a mess!"

"You had a draft colt in there . . ."

He cut me off before I could finish. "That damn colt!" (Del was bishop of his ward that year, so it was significant that he would swear.) "I have three pregnant mares. What the hell am I going to do with a bunch of half-draft colts!" He rambled on for a while, adding more colorful words as he listed his frustrations with the situation. Eventually, he wound down and asked, "Why do you ask"?

"Well, that answers my question," I said. "It looks like that little brown mare I board for Stacy is going to have a colt too. I'll let her know what's up."

Stacy and her parents were not too upset when I confirmed what I suspected. They wanted to know if Swifty would be okay since the foal's sire was a draft horse, and Swifty was small even for a Quarter Horse. I explained that, unlike cows, horses don't usually have a problem with foals that are too big.

They kept her in the pasture for a couple more months. I didn't have the space to keep an extra mare and colt since we had a couple of mares that were going to foal too, so they arranged to take her to another place. I hauled Swifty over to Blaine and Nancy's stable for her, and when the mare was settled in the new corral, I said, "What are you going to do with the colt?"

"We want to keep it!" Stacy said, surprised that I asked.

I told her, "No, you really don't, colts are a pain in the butt. They really are."

"Oh, I'm sure it will be fine, we want to keep it," she assured me.

I said, "Okay, give me a call if you change your mind." I was engaged to be married that summer. Robert was a big guy, and I had been thinking a half draft colt would be the right size for him. "We'll buy him from you if you end up wanting to sell him."

"Okay, we'll call you if we change our minds, but I'm sure we will keep him," Stacy replied.

On the Fourth of July, I got a call from Stacy. She was very excited and told me Swifty had foaled, and she and the foal were fine. The colt was chestnut with three stocking legs and a big blaze on his face. Stacy was full of questions about what to do next and how to take care of the colt. I answered her questions and told her Blaine and Nancy would know what to do if she had any trouble.

Four months later, I got a call from Stacy. "Do you still want that colt?" she asked.

"Yes, we'd like to have him, we have an orphan that needs a friend," I replied. Our mare, Rose, had died a few hours after her filly was born. We named the filly Bonnie and were raising her by hand. She thought she was a human and really needed another horse to live with. "What changed your mind?"

"He's chasing us out of the corral and won't stay in anywhere! You were right, colts are obnoxious." She then went on to list his various exploits, adding, "He turns his butt to us and kicks at us when we try to catch him."

"Well, how much would you like for him?" I asked.

"How about $200," she said.

"Sounds like a great deal to me, we'll come get him," I replied.

It was already November, and since the mare had the colt so late, he wasn't getting much use out of the mare's milk anyway. Swifty looked no worse for wear when we got there. Oddly enough, although Stacy had the mare bred many times after that, it took over twelve years to get another colt out of her.

Everyone who met Clyde assumed his name was Clyde because he's part Clydesdale, but actually, he got that name because Bonnie and Clyde were so much trouble.

It didn't take us long to teach Clyde some manners, but he and Bonnie were always finding things to play with, including people who happened into their corral. Luckily, we had Bob around to show us how to keep Clyde from getting the upper hand. He knew how to teach horses good manners.

My new husband was not a horse person, but he came in handy a couple of times with Clyde. Clyde had only been at our place for a day or two when Robert went down to the barn to help feed. Clyde promptly spun around and threatened to kick him. Robert began to move out of the way, then he thought to himself, "What would Bob do?" So he smacked Clyde on the butt with the empty bucket in his hand, then chased the colt out of the barn. That was the end of Clyde kicking at people.

The second time was when we were teaching Clyde to lead. Being a half draft horse, Clyde was a big colt. At six months old, he was almost fifteen hands high, and he was built stout. Robert was oversized too—he was built like an NFL defensive end. When Clyde balked and didn't want to lead, Robert just kept going. Clyde's hooves made skid marks in the corral dirt, but he couldn't outpull Robert. He gave up after only a few feet and led like a gentleman after that.

THE ESCAPE ARTIST

Clyde was so adept at escaping and causing other kinds of mischief that the people I worked with in my "normal" job—as in not at the barn—began asking me, "What has Clyde done lately?" or "What did Clyde do this weekend?" He was the only horse we owned that practically everyone I worked with knew by name. He was also a fun source of icebreaker stories for the classes I taught.

Clyde assumed gate latches and tied lead ropes were there as a nice puzzle the silly humans left for him to solve. We had to replace all the gate latches at Bob's place and ours with chains so he couldn't get them open. When playing with the latches didn't work anymore, he jumped over. He rarely left, though; he'd wait around until someone noticed him and put him back in. His goal was to solve the puzzle, not to escape.

We resorted to an electric fence at the top of the fences, since he soon learned to step on the wire and walk over. The electric fences only lasted about a month. If it was too much effort to jump out, he'd squish the mesh fence and shimmy under the electric one.

It's dangerous to picket horses; they tend to panic and scar up their legs with rope burns. But out of sheer desperation, we finally put him on a picket rope until we had built a corral that would actually keep him in. It's a good thing Robert was an accomplished welder.

The fences around the barn are made of drill pipe welded together and cemented into the ground. All because of Clyde. Robert's dad helped us build the barn and fences, and one day he took on the task of hanging the gate to the pasture. We designed them so there were two posts next to each other so you could walk through without having to open the gate. They were too narrow for a horse to get through. Robert's dad made sure the posts were perfectly straight and that the gate swung free and level. Clyde stood nearby and watched him the whole time.

As soon as Robert's dad was done setting the posts, he walked away and Clyde ambled up to the hole in the fence.

Robert said, "Ha, we've got you this time, Clyde."

Clyde stuck his head through the walk-through posts and looked around. Then he shifted his shoulders so they were both even against the posts, took a stance so his back legs would have the most pushing power, and shoved.

He tilted the posts out enough that we had to put wire on the top to take the V out, and the gate has never swung level since.

You can just imagine the words Robert and his dad used that day.

***

Clyde got stuck in the fence when he was a yearling and cut his ankle quite severely. After that, if he got wrapped in wire badly enough that he couldn't escape by himself, he'd wait for someone to come find him. Most horses will panic and hurt themselves even worse if a fence wire wraps around their ankle since they're trapped in the fence and can't get away. He never did get cut again, no matter how many barbed wire or field fences he ended up ensnared in.

About when we thought he was done getting caught in fences because we had replaced or built new ones all around our farm to pass the Clyde test, he fell in love with a mare down the road. All the normal gates were Clyde-proof by then, so he decided to take the direct approach to get to her: right through a pile of rolled-up fence and farm machinery our neighbor had heaped up in the corner of his field.

We were hanging around the barn doing horse stuff, and all the pasture horses except Clyde had come up to see what we were doing. We noticed Clyde standing in the far corner of the field by himself. He was independent, so that wasn't unusual. And the field is a quarter mile long, so we couldn't tell what side of the fence he was on. A couple of the 4-H kids were there with me. We rode some horses in the arena, and by the time we were done, it was nearing lunchtime. Still, Clyde hadn't moved. I thought maybe we should go check things out. I took a pair of wire cutters with me just in case.

When we got down there, Clyde was standing with all four legs in barbed wire and field fence up to his belly. There was an old hay rake in the pile too, and a tine was tight enough against his ribs that it was making a dent. I couldn't imagine how we were supposed to get him out of that mess without him tearing his legs up. Most horses would absolutely freak out in a spot like that, and when you try to help them, they start trying to move on their own and hurt themselves worse.

I started cutting wire, and the girls would move it away. It was a good five minutes before we could even free one leg. We shifted his leg, and he left it where we put it. Then we cut and pulled some more.

I was really scared when we got the first leg free because a normal horse will think if one leg is free, surely if they struggle, they can get out of that trap. Of course, what they end up doing is shredding their legs.

Not Clyde. He left each leg exactly where we put it until all that was left was the chunk of farm machinery. It took all three of us to pull the pile of fence out of the way. Then I walked up to him and asked him to step sideways. He sidled over until he could step over the rake and *voila!* He was free. All he got out of that mess was a couple of tiny nicks. I'm sure any other horse would have needed stitches.

Luckily, Del moved the mare to another pasture shortly after, and Clyde quit trying to get to her.

THE FEED SACK

Good old Clyde.

One hazard with horses that escape is that if they get into any grain, they will eat too much and get sick, sometimes sick enough to kill them or destroy their feet. They get a high fever, and it shows up as founder (laminitis) in their hooves. Clyde got out countless times, and even doorknobs barely slowed him down, so the first time he got into the feed, he overate and foundered. Luckily, his feet recovered. He never overate again, no matter how many times he got into the tack room where the grain was.

That is highly unusual in a horse. Since it can take several hours for overeating to cause them to get sick, most horses don't associate what they ate with being sick. They live entirely in the moment. Clyde was not that way. He was a mule in horse clothing. He could associate the past with his present, and he could plan. Which leads me to the oddest thing Clyde ever did.

Horses are programmed to be spooky and leery of things that wave or flutter or are an unusual color. Predators do eat them, so it's not that strange that they are like that. My husband was fond of saying, "I don't know why anyone was worried about a cavalry charge, all you'd have to do is have someone stand on a hill with a couple white sheets and wait for them to charge, then wave the bedsheets at them." The thing is, anyone who has owned a horse will tell you he's not too far off with that idea.

One day, when Clyde was older, probably about ten, I was fiddling around in the tack room. It was almost time to feed, so the pasture horses were coming into the catch pen to wait for me to toss them hay. I wasn't paying attention to them, but I did hear them walk into the corral, and then moments later they would all bolt and tear off down the field. I heard that a couple of times and decided I should go see what was up.

Clyde was standing in the far corner of the catch pen, facing away from the pasture gate. He was holding very still with his head down and had his left ear pricked toward the gate. Generally, a horse's ear will point the way their eye is looking, and they can see almost all the way around their body. They actually see two images at once most of the time, so he was looking behind himself at the gate, waiting for the other horses to come into the catch pen.

In his mouth was a white feed sack that must have blown into the corral. I *swear* he had a wicked grin on his face while he waited for all the horses to file into the corral. When the last horse was in, Clyde spun around, feed sack in his mouth, stomped with his front feet, and shook the sack.

Horses spooked, snorted, spun around, and ran into each other in a pell-mell race to get away from the scary sack.

If horses could laugh, Clyde would have been rolling on the ground.

I laughed too, but not as hard as I might have. The thing was, that little scene was almost spooky to me. Horses simply aren't supposed to be able to think like that.

THE "GOOD OLD BOY"

Clyde eventually became christened a "good old boy," which is Bob-speak for an exceptionally reliable horse. Although he was unusually intelligent for a horse, he was not mean, and he liked people.

Smart horses, by the way, are often the most dangerous and obnoxious of horses. They don't want to go along with what people want them to do and can come up with all kinds of ways to get out of work. Before they began breeding horses for bucking, the most common bucking horses were riding lesson horses that had learned all kinds of tricks to buck people off. Bucking horses, after all, only have to work about five minutes a year. In fact, I tell people if I came back as a horse, I'd want to be a bucking horse. I would get to buck people off in all kinds of exotic ways, I'd get to travel around the country, and I'd get to hang out with a bunch of pasture mates doing nothing the rest of the time.

Clyde bucked only three times in his life. Once was the first time he was saddled. After he bucked around the corral and the saddle didn't come off, Clyde decided that was too much work and didn't try it again.

The second time I've already recounted—when he was supposed to be carrying that gravestone into the ranch.

The third time was when he was in his teens. Kaytee, who was one of the kids in my 4-H group, needed a horse to ride for the pre-rodeo show at the Box Elder Fair. She asked if she could borrow Clyde, so I agreed. The 4-H demonstration game that day were team pole bending—they set up two sets of poles and pit one rider against another to see who can weave in and out of them the fastest.

Clyde was usually not bothered by crowds and noise. We had driven him in parades many times and even through a hailstorm once, and he took it all in stride. Kaytee had ridden him a few times before and was a good rider, but she could tell the crowd and the noise from the loudspeakers were bothering him.

Soon, it was her turn to go. Kaytee kicked Clyde into a gallop, and he started out. He was a big horse and had a big stride. In addition, his lope was the rocking-horse kind: you went up and down a lot. Kaytee liked to ride jumping horses as well, so it took a few strides for her to realize Clyde's leaps were getting higher.

A couple of strides more and Clyde decided the noise and loudspeaker squawking was too much for him. He started all-out bucking. Kaytee stayed on clear to the end of the poles, then bailed off. The announcer said she would have gotten at least a 90 score for that ride.

For some odd reason, none of the 4-H kids borrowed Clyde for the pre-rodeo show after that.

Clyde in the Box Elder Fair parade, 1998.

GREEN RIDERS

If you ask someone if they can ride, most will say yes. But these days, most people don't get a chance to learn to ride well. It's hard to explain to them that most horses are not safe for the average person to ride. They assume that if you can ride a horse, then surely they can, too, which simply isn't true.

It helps to have a good old horse around that you can put anyone on and they'll be taken care of. Clyde ended up being one of those. He thought green riders were entertaining.

If friends or relatives came over and wanted to ride, I'd put them on Clyde and then I'd lead the way on the trail up to the canal. I wanted to be in front because then I didn't have to watch what Clyde did. They would be safe with him, but he made sure they paid for making him work.

When an experienced rider was on him, he'd outwalk almost any horse. His trot was also nice and fairly smooth when his rider cared about him doing things right. And if there were jumps around, he wanted to try the biggest one. But with green riders, it was a different story.

There was often quite a string of riders of various skill levels following me through the orchards as we wound our way up the hill. We'd usually get about halfway through the orchard, and Clyde's rider would holler to wait up. He would be at the back of the line, coming along at a snail's pace. I'd turn my horse around and watch while Clyde ambled up the road, pausing to get a mouthful of grass as he went. I'd tell them to slap him with their reins and say "trot," and Clyde would shuffle along with the bumpiest slow trot he could manage while his rider's head and arms flopped around until they caught up. Then we'd head out again.

When we got to the canal road, he took great delight in tight-roping the edge on the downhill side rather than walking in the middle of the road. The more the riders tugged at his reins to get him off that perilous side, the more he hugged the very edge. Then, for good measure, he'd reach down over the brow of the hill every so often and pull up a grass clump, which meant his head and neck disappeared and his rider was looking out into open space.

Sometimes I'd have pity on them and take one of Clyde's reins to lead him along for a while, but usually I pretended I didn't hear them splutter.

If Clyde ended up in the middle of the string of horses, he would torture the horses behind him by creeping along, slow-like, and cutting them off when they'd try to pass him. They rarely dared to push past because Clyde was the boss of the pasture. His rider, not knowing it was all a plot of Clyde's, would complain that they couldn't get him to walk a straight line.

When we got to a log to cross, he'd stand there while they thumped their heels on his side and clucked at him. When they seemed to be running out of steam, he'd climb over or, better yet, do a little bunny hop so his rider would get a good jolt. This was the same horse who, with a rider experienced at jumping, would charge at the biggest jump he could find and sail over in good form when we took him to the cross-country course. He would jump anything he was pointed at if you let him.

KILLER SHEEP

My husband and I had each other over a barrel. We both had expensive addictions. Mine was horses, and his was birds. It worked out well. But one summer, when I was pregnant with our second child, Robert decided he would use Clyde for hunting. He had not ridden Clyde very much, but I told him if he wanted to do that, he'd have to get the horse in shape, and I'd be glad to show him what to do.

His friend Ken was another bird guy, but he'd ridden horses as a kid, so he knew what he was about, and we let him use my brown mare named Noble. They started riding the horses up the hill, and Jennifer, who was nine years old that summer, would go with them. I'm not certain, but she had probably spent more time in the saddle at her young age than either of the two men.

Eventually, they got things sorted out and took the two horses to a spot Bob knew where they could fill their deer tags. Ken, Bob, and Robert unloaded the horses and began to tie them to the trailer. Bob was busy getting the camp set up. He left the other two to take care of the horses. Next thing he knew, he heard a clatter of horse hooves on gravel, lots of cursing, and turned to see Robert pelting down the road on foot. It turned out Clyde, being Clyde, had untied himself and decided to go for a run. He took Noble with him since Ken hadn't finished tying her up yet. She ripped the rope out of Ken's hands and followed her leader down the gravel road and out of sight around a bend.

Ken and Bob unhooked the trailer, grabbed a can full of grain and a lariat, and went to find them. First, they came upon Robert limping along down the road. He had rocks in his boots. He thought the horses would head for the paved road toward home, but they'd passed that by and kept going along the gravel one, so none of them could figure where the horses would go since neither of the horses had been to that spot in the past.

They drove on the road a ways and asked at a few campsites. Sure enough, they'd all seen the two horses and pointed in the direction they'd gone.

About the time Bob was commenting that they couldn't be too much farther since Clyde was too lazy to keep running, they rounded another bend in the road, and there they were, heading straight for the truck, going back toward the horse trailer. They didn't even hesitate at the truck; they just went around, one on each side, eyes wide with fear.

Everyone was surprised. Noble was normal and could talk herself into being spooked rather easily. Clyde, on the other hand, was rarely truly afraid of things. The three men exchanged looks and turned the truck around.

When they got back to camp, Clyde and Noble were standing at the trailer, sides heaving, waiting for their humans to come take care of them. About ten minutes later, a guy showed up on a four-wheeler to see if the horses were okay. He said he was talking to a sheepherder whose herd was crossing the road when the two horses came around the bend and ran into the herd. Clyde and Noble took one look at those scary, stinky, wooly things and decided the horse trailer was a much safer option. Although both of them had seen sheep before, they'd never been up close and personal with them.

SAM THE
SCHOOLMASTER

When Clyde was two, we were still racing chariot horses and needed a draft horse to teach the colts to drive. Bob put the word out to his horse buddies, and eventually, we found Sam. Sam had been used as a show horse and for pulling wagons for the Seiferts, the family that sold breeding stock for the Budweiser Clydesdales. They couldn't use Sam anymore because he had been string-halted, which is a term for nerve damage in the hind legs from pulling too hard. Sam was 18.2 hands high (a "hand" is four inches, so he was six feet two inches tall at the withers) and had the classic Clydesdale look. He was bay with a bald face and stocking legs complete with feathers. He was good and quiet and perfect for what we needed. It was fall when we bought him, and we set him to work getting our current colt team ready to race.

He was a good old boy and was unconcerned if the colts got a little excited. No matter how much you prepare, when you hook a horse to a chariot or cart the first time, you never really know what to expect. Some of them understand it's the next step. Others lose their minds since that thing is following them, and they feel trapped because they're attached to it. They'll try to bolt, or buck, or hang back. With a big horse like Sam, it doesn't really matter what the regular-size horse does. If you asked Sam to go left, they would both go left; if you asked Sam to go forward, they would both go forward, even if the colt was sitting on his butt or bouncing off the chariot tongue.

We hooked Clyde up with Sam. Clyde was smart enough that

he was not concerned about the chariot. It wasn't long before we could drive him in a cart by himself or on a wagon with Sam. The only problem was that it only took two blocks pulling the wagon for Clyde to figure out he could get Sam to pull the whole thing. All he did was hold the tongue up. You'd be driving along, and Clyde would look pretty pulling with Sam, but if you looked at the tugs (the straps that pull the wagon), they'd be hanging loose.

That spring and summer, we drove the wagon around town and even in a couple of parades. Clyde took it all in stride. He was never bothered by parades. Sam was unconcerned too; he was a typical draft horse: born broke.

MIDNIGHT RUN

Sam's gallop was about the speed of a regular horse's slow trot. One night, I had just crawled into bed and turned the lights off when the windows began to rattle, and I heard a horse trotting past the bedroom. It had to be Sam to be that loud. I put some jeans and a jacket on and went out to see what was up. All of the horses in the upper pasture had escaped, and it looked like they were heading for Perry, the town north of us. That week, I had begun boarding two new mares named Ella and Misty that used to live in Perry. They were heading home, taking the rest of the horses with them.

I hollered at Robert, called Bob, and headed for the barn for halters and grain. It took us about ten minutes to gather things together and come up with a game plan. I was stepping into the truck when I heard horses coming down the road. They galloped down our lane, dashed past us, and ran back into the pasture. That was by far the easiest horse roundup I had ever been on. A man in a small car followed them down the lane. He said he was turning onto the KOA road in Perry when these horses almost hit his car. It was too dark to see them coming. He said the horses stopped, turned around, and took off heading south. My big bay mare, BC, had decided to go home and headed back to Willard, taking the rest of the crowd with her since she was the boss.

We counted the horses, and they all appeared to be there. We stood around, chatting about how lucky we were and how great it was that nobody got hurt. Then the guy from Perry left, and Bob went home. Robert and I did another check on the pasture gate, then headed for the house. We had almost made it to our driveway when Sam appeared out of the dark doing a slow shuffle. I guess that was his version of a fast trot. Poor old Sam. It had taken him that long to get back to our place! We had forgotten about him.

HIT THE FLY

Sam the babysitter.

When spring turned into summer the first year we had Sam, we found out a funny quirk about him. Draft horse tails are cut off short (docked) because it's too dangerous for them to have a big, heavy tail. It's easy for a horse to flip their tail over the driving lines, and if their tail is too heavy, you can't get the lines back out from under. So, their tails are docked when they are foals. That means their tail is too short to swish at flies.

This is what Sam would do to unsuspecting people. Picture yourself walking across a wide-open pasture. You see a big horse in the distance, trotting around. The horse turns and spots you. He starts heading your way at a gallop. As he gets nearer, you realize this horse is taller than you are. The ground begins to shake; his feet are the size of dinner plates. He is headed straight at you. You look around. There is nowhere to run, nothing to get behind. You believe you are doomed. This giant horse is going to squish you. Then, when he is one stride away, he spins around and puts his massive butt right in your face.

You're supposed to hit the horsefly.

Incidentally, that's the only time Sam would gallop voluntarily.

At 18.2 hands high, Sam was as tall as a six-foot man at his withers (the base of his neck). He weighed almost a ton. We once got ten kids sitting on him from behind his ears to his tail. He was content as long as he got a good scratch and someone hit the horseflies for him.

PALE FACE ANNIE

One of Bob's broodmares was named Pale Face Annie. Her sire was a horse named Pale Face Joe. She was racehorse bred and was what you'd call extra-large for a Quarter Horse. She stood about 16.2 hands (5'4" at the withers) and probably weighed 1500 pounds. She was not only tall but wide and stout. She was dark brown with a big, bald face.

Broodmares are often cranky, and Annie was no exception. She had a couple of funny quirks about her. If you tied her solid to something, she would do everything in her power to get away, and she had a *lot* of power. She would stand there good if you just looped the rope over the rail, but not if it was tight. She loaded in a trailer the same way. If you walked up to the trailer and stood there and waited for a minute or two, she would walk right in, but if you tried to pull her in, she would fight.

We were told she got that way because when she was a colt, she hung back and the rope went tight and jerked her forward into the end of a pipe she was tied to. It made a big hole in her chest. She still had the scar when we got her, so she was convinced tight ropes were a bad thing. Now, things like that can be fixed if you're persistent and willing to risk getting yourself and the horse hurt, but Bob knew that sometimes it's best to leave things be.

We were trading colts with Doyle. He had a nice stallion, and he would breed a couple of our mares to his stud and we would get the colts, and the next year he would get to keep the colts. The first time we took Annie to Doyle's, Bob explained how to load her in a trailer and not to tie her solid to anything. Doyle was often as cranky as an old broodmare and said, "I won't put up with that sort of thing! I can handle it."

Bob said, "I really wouldn't try to fix that mare if I was you, but you do what you want."

A couple of weeks later, we were driving past Doyle's place and saw quite a scene there. Doyle's pickup and two-horse trailer were blocking the whole road. Apparently, he had tied Annie to the trailer and tried to make her go in. The only reason she had stopped dragging the truck and trailer backwards was because there was a big irrigation ditch behind her on the opposite side of the road from Doyle's place. She might hang back like a crazy horse, but she wasn't stupid.

I asked Bob if we should stop and help Doyle. He said, "No, he can handle it."

The other funny quirk Annie had was chasing people for fun. As I said, she was a really big mare. At the time, I had only seen Annie up in the Huntsville pasture, which was where we usually kept the broodmares. We had only recently moved in with Bob in the Clinton house. Behind our property was a large pasture that Bob and his chariot buddy, Ogden, rented from a friend. It was the pasture I galloped the racehorses in.

The pasture was on the corner with a subdivision behind it. At the far end of the pasture was the bus stop. The school kids would climb over the fence and walk across the pasture as a shortcut. Bob wouldn't have minded that, except they were breaking the fence down, making it low enough that it was a hazard to the horses.

After a couple of weeks of fixing the squished fence, Bob thought of Annie. I went with him to get her. On the way home, he explained that if a stranger went out in the pasture with Annie, she would run at them with her mouth wide open. He said all you had to do was stand there, and she would just stop or run right past when she got to you if you didn't move. But if you ran, she would stay right behind you all the way to the fence. He knew I hadn't been around horses very much yet, so he said if it was too scary to stand there, bring a bucket and swing it at her when she got close. He assured me it would only take once, and if I didn't run away, she would not try to chase me again. He said she never had touched anyone when she chased them.

Sure enough, the first time I walked out there, Annie came for me. I don't care who you are, a massive horse running at you with their ears flat and mouth open is a scary sight. I had brought a bucket with me like Bob told me to, and when she was a few feet away, I swung the bucket and yelled—the yelling was my own invention, not Bob's suggestion. I was *scared*. The bucket tagged her on the shoulder when she came by. I stood still, but not because Bob told me to—I don't think my legs would have worked at that point. I didn't know it then, but in the horse world, the one who doesn't move is the boss. Annie turned back and looked at me for a few seconds then walked away, completely ignoring me.

Well, the school kids didn't know Annie was all bluff. It only took a couple of days, and the pasture was a kid-free zone. No more fixing squished fences.

THE BURGER BAR

Bob's friend Orluff ran chariot horses with him for a few years. Orluff was a nice guy and enjoyed the horses, but he was new to owning them. He and Bob kept their broodmares on Orluff's pasture up in the "Valley," as everyone around here calls the mountain valley the town of Huntsville sits in.

Orluff was brilliant when it came to finance and running a construction business, but he was new to the farm life. One day, Bob went to get one of the mares out of the pasture, and Orluff had chained the gate shut and locked it with a padlock. He didn't tell Bob he did it, but he'd heard of some horses being stolen in the Valley, so he locked the gate to keep them safe.

Bob knew Orluff would be off somewhere at a job site and too hard to find, so he just lifted the gate off the hinges and got the mare out. Then he put the gate back on the hinges. This was before cell phones, so he didn't call Orluff to tell him he'd taken the mare. He thought he would call when he got done running around that day. After all, it was Bob's mare that he took out of the pasture, and it was time she went to the breeder's.

When Bob got home later that day, Mom met him at the door. Orluff had called in a panic to tell her someone had stolen Bob's horse! He'd locked the gate and couldn't figure out how someone had gotten in and taken her, or why she was only one that was gone.

Orluff was both relieved and annoyed at Bob when he found out who had "stolen" the horse. He commented, "What if I put a lock on the other side of the gate too!"

Without missing a beat, Bob said, "Then I'd just undo the wire fence and get her out that way."

Orluff sighed and gave up his side of the argument.

***

If you've ever watched the movie *The Electric Horseman*, the horse in it was actually a cutting horse, not a racehorse. A cutting horse is a horse trained to sort cattle. Robert Redford liked cutting horses and chose Noel Skinner as his trainer, who was the best around at training cutting and reining horses in our part of the country back then. The horse in the movie went on to win top honors in the national cutting horse scene.

Orluff's daughter and Bob's Uncle Doug's boy both had horses in training with Noel at the same time, so Orluff got to know the actor. One day, he had quite the story to tell Bob.

Paul Newman happened to be visiting with his friend Robert at Noel's place. When they got done practicing with the horses at Noel's barn, they were hungry. Orluff asked what they liked, and they said a burger would be good. Orluff told them the best place to get a burger was at the Burger Bar, which was true. They agreed, and he drove them out there.

The place was crowded, as usual, and the line at the window was long. Orluff pulled up close enough to read the menu, and they decided on what they wanted. Redford got out to order their food. When he reached the window and began to order, Newman told Orluff to drive off. He'd taken Redford's wallet. Orluff played along, and they circled the block, chuckling. Apparently, playing tricks on each other was a common thing.

When they got back to the Burger Bar, Orluff got out to go pay for the food, and he could hear Redford arguing with the girl at the window. He was telling the girl who he was and insisting that his friend had pulled a dirty trick on him.

The girl rolled her eyes and said, "Uh-huh," in a "what do you think I am, an idiot?" tone.

About then, Redford caught sight of Orluff as he stepped up to the window. He was red in the face from embarrassment, and the crowd near the window had gotten larger. They were all shaking their heads at the crazy man trying to get out of paying. He said, "This guy will tell you. Orluff, tell her who I am."

Orluff put on his best "What?" look and tried to hide his snicker.

Redford said, "Oh, come on!"

Newman must have decided Redford had suffered enough, because he walked up beside Orluff, having parked the car down the road.

The girl at the window hadn't recognized Redford, even in his cowboy boots and button-down shirt when he was all alone—but seeing the two actors together could not be denied. She went pale, dropped her pen, and clutched the counter for support. She began gushing apologies and turned redder in the face than Redford had been.

Redford was a good sport, and they soon went on their way.

Bob and Orluff ran chariot horses together for a few years, but then Orluff's business got successful enough that he could buy better racehorses than Bob could afford. About then, Bob decided to move to racing at the Golden Spike track in Brigham instead of the Wasatch Slopes track where he and Orluff ran, so they stopped racing chariot teams together.

They remained good friends.

KATIE ADAMS

Katie Adams was born to be a momma. She *loved* foals—any foal. She also produced above average racehorses. In that same pasture up in Huntsville, Bob had five broodmares along with their colts. It was the year we moved in with Bob. He took me with him to get Katie out since one of the mares was due to foal.

On the way there, I asked, "Why are we going to pick up Katie if she's not the one having the colt?"

"'Cause she'll steal the other mare's foal. That'll cause her to foal early, and her own colt won't get the colostrum it needs to survive."

Well, I was new to this horse thing and only understood about half of what he said, and it wasn't the important part. I said, "Huh?"

He chuckled and explained, "Colostrum is the first milk a newborn animal drinks. It's full of antibodies that help the foal fight infections and disease, but it only lasts a couple days."

"Oh." I contemplated that for a minute or two, then said, "I thought mares don't adopt colts."

Bob knew I'd read every book I could get my hands on about horses, so he said, "Katie doesn't read books."

The pasture up in Huntsville was more than ten acres, and there weren't any smaller pens in it. Katie might not read books, but she could read people quite well. Plus, she was smarter than the average mare. As soon as we stepped into the pasture, she hightailed it for the other end. She knew Bob was there to get her and wasn't about to make it easy for him.

Bob pretended he didn't want her and set out some buckets with grain in them. The other horses came over to get some grain, and he took out a brush and started brushing their coats and set me to combing out their manes. He said to ignore Katie. We hung out there for a while, and she eventually wandered over our way.

Bob walked away. The other horses followed him until he got to the fence. He got a little more grain and climbed back in the pasture, then handed me a bucket and a hay string. He said, "Shake this out on the ground in a line, then come back and scratch their shoulders when you do. When you get to Katie, slip this string around her neck."

It took us about fifteen minutes in all to catch Katie that day. But once I got to know her, there were times when other people would go to catch her without Bob, and it would take them an hour or more.

Once Katie had her own colt, she didn't steal someone else's, but she'd let any colt nurse. Since she was the boss mare of the pasture, it seemed that she set an example. Three of the five mares in there started letting any colt nurse that wanted to. It was a free-for-all milk parlor. Katie only tolerated humans, but when it came to foals, she would have adopted them all if she could have.

Later that summer, Bob put Cutty Sark in the pasture with her and the other mares. Cutty was a yearling. When he came back to check on them a couple of weeks later, Katie was letting Cutty nurse too! We ended up having to wean both her foal *and* her yearling that fall.

LIFE LESSONS

There's more to owning horses than the critters themselves. They are great teachers, especially for kids. There's nothing like a horse to teach a kid the value of love without judgment, as well as patience and certainly humility. Adults have a harder time learning those lessons than kids. I know I constantly have to work on those qualities. Horses are great at knocking a person down a peg, and that's a good thing.

COPPER

When we lived in Clinton, our neighbor had a big bay horse named Copper. Copper was not the brightest horse, and he tended to overreact to things. They also had a pair of Toulouse geese—the big ornery gray and white ones. The pair made a nest and had finally built a nice clutch of eggs. They mostly ignored Copper since they arrived the previous fall. In the days leading up to this event, they paid no attention to Copper as they assembled their nest and laid the eggs, but once the clutch of eggs was laid, suddenly the gander believed Copper was a threat.

Poor Copper had no idea the rules had changed. He wandered over to see what the geese were up to, and the gander decided that was too close to their nest. He hissed and charged. Copper wheeled around and started to trot away, but not fast enough to lose the goose. The goose grabbed a big bite of tail in his beak and hung on. Copper saw that thing on the end of his tail and took off in a flat-out run.

It was a half-acre pasture, and Copper made three laps in record time with that old gander flapping away at the back. Copper would slide at the corners, and the goose would swing out to the side, nearly hitting the fence, but he kept his grip.

We were all standing at the fence by then, trying to breathe with tears in our eyes from laughing, and wondering how this was going to end. Finally, Copper's tail hairs came out. The goose was not ready for the sudden drop in speed, and he landed in a heap and did a couple of somersaults, feathers, tail hairs, and dirt flying. The gander got up squawking and staggered back to his nest.

Copper was so dingy anyway we couldn't tell if the incident made him any worse, but he left that piece of pasture alone. He wouldn't even sneak a bite of grass in that corner until the chicks had grown enough to move elsewhere.

TONTO

Bob didn't know show horse stuff. His interest was racehorses and saddle horses. He didn't worry about things like what lead a horse was on, or if their headset was correct. Bob had another kind of knowledge, a much rarer kind. He was a true horseman. He understood how horses thought. He treated them like horses, not like prize poodles or an object to use for winning prizes.

When we moved in with him, I had read every book I could find about horses, so I thought I knew stuff. A neighbor let my friend and me ride her mare bareback for a quarter a ride. Cindy and I spent most of two summers doing chores to earn quarters. I thought I knew something about horses. Bob could see in a moment I really didn't. But since he figured a girl could ride and handle horses as well as a boy, he was glad to have a kid living there who wanted to help him out with his racehorses. I figured I was the luckiest fourteen-year-old ever.

To start me out learning how to ride well, he bought me Tonto. Tonto was a tall, lanky sorrel gelding. He had a nice hip and a good, long neck, but otherwise, he was not the prettiest beast—or "butt-ugly" as Bob put it when speaking of Tonto. He was a good broke horse on the lazy side. The perfect horse for a kid to learn to ride on. Tonto was a very good teacher.

For instance, when it was a scary or dangerous spot, he would watch every step and take you carefully to the other side of whatever it was. But when you were riding along a good flat road, he would trip every few steps, not bothering to watch his feet. Once, he even walked right into a mailbox. I was turned around, undoing my jacket from the saddle strings. I guess he figured it was my job to look where we were going.

Like a lot of lazy horses, he was smarter than most. He had figured out people would pamper him and quit riding if he limped. If you were going somewhere he didn't want to, or if he was getting tired, he would limp. The limp would get worse the farther you went. We could tell he was faking because if something distracted him, he would forget which leg he was limping on and switch to the other one.

Years later, we sold him to our friend Danny, and he took him hunting. It was three days into the deer hunt before Danny figured out Tonto really was limping and not faking it. He felt quite guilty, but Bob told him, "That's what the old horse gets for crying wolf."

Tonto was an escape artist. We had an elaborate setup at the barn in Clinton to keep him out of the grain. We kept adding things to block him from getting in, and he kept outfoxing us. He could turn the handles on the stall doors, so we put a chain on them. That fooled him for a while, but eventually, he figured out how to trap the snap on the chain so he could get it undone. Then we tied ropes from the hitch rail to the gate where the grain bin was kept, but he crawled under. So we put a gate there, too.

That stumped him for a few days. Then he figured out another path. He would squeeze between the hitch rail and the wall and duck down so his back wouldn't hit the shelves with the grooming tools on them. Then he would open the gate to the hay and grain and go have some to eat.

If a horse eats too much grain all at once, they will founder and often end up ruining their feet, so we didn't dare let him stay in there. One of us would spot him from the house. We would usually be in the kitchen. There wasn't room for him to turn around. He had to back out.

Most horses will panic if they're caught in a small space. Not Tonto. As soon as he heard the door open and us come out of the house, he'd start backing up, being very careful but not wasting any time, and scoot through that narrow gap backwards—he had to squish his sides to fit. He would remember to bend down so he didn't bump himself on the shelves, too.

As soon as his shoulders were clear of the hitch rail, he would spin around and run away. He would always get out before we could catch him.

What I learned from Tonto, in addition to how to ride, was that horses understand kindness and patience, too. He was an excellent teacher for a green kid. A "good, honest horse," as Bob would say.

WILLY

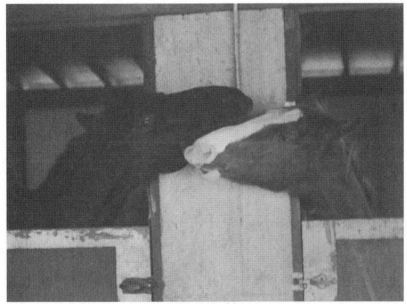

Willy & Buddy.

The second horse Bob got for me to ride was an entirely different story. I had decided I wanted to learn to ride English and jump horses. Tonto wasn't built very well for that sort of thing, so Bob asked around and found a horse named Willy. He was a tall, black Thoroughbred that had a little more muscle than most Thoroughbreds. He had done well as a racehorse and had been kept as a stallion until he was seven. I forget what his registered name was. Willy stood for Will-He. As in "will he or won't he buck?".

He had absolutely *no* manners, but he *loved* to jump. He would go around and jump the jumps by himself if we left them up, and that's why Bob bought him. He figured if I wanted to learn to be a horse trainer, Willy would be the best teacher for that. Mostly, what horse trainers get sent to them are either totally untrained colts or older horses with behavior problems. Willy had quite a lot of issues, so even though he was an excellent jumper, he was cheap. Bob told people he bought the saddle for $1,000 and the horse for $500.

Bob proceeded to show me how to teach Willy manners.

Many of Willy's habits were downright dangerous. The first one Bob chose to address was taking off when he was turned loose. Willy would aim a kick at you as he jerked his head out of the halter. The horse's previous owners had believed he needed understanding and kindness. What he needed was a good kick in the ass a couple of times. He was like the kid who turns into a bully because no one at home makes them mind.

Bob tied a long lariat to the stout post that the pasture gate hung on. Then he got Willy out and put a rope halter on first. Over the top of that, he put a flat halter and regular lead. Bob had me stand to the side so I wouldn't get kicked, then as they passed the gate, he clipped that lariat to the rope halter.

Bob began to undo the flat halter, and Willy got ready to take off. Bob commanded, "Stand still!" Willy ignored him and pranced around. Bob turned Willy so he was facing the gate, not the pasture, and wouldn't have room to kick him when he spun around to run. Then he slipped the halter off Willy's nose and said, "Whoa!" Willy took off.

He got about four good strides in, and Bob said, "Whoa!" right before Willy hit the end of the lariat. The ground was muddy and soft since it was spring. Willy was jerked around sideways and landed flat on his side with a loud thump.

Willy was far from stupid. When Bob said "whoa" after that, he stopped and stood there like a gentleman.

The next goal Bob had was to show me how to teach Willy ground manners. Willy would drag people around when he was excited about going somewhere, and he'd stand like a mule when he didn't want to go. It only took minutes for him to lead well for Bob. The horse knew when he was outsmarted. It took a while longer for him to listen to me; he wasn't convinced I was worth his respect. Eventually, he got good enough that Bob would let me handle and ride him by myself. He told me, "One of these days, you're going to have it out with that horse, and if you win, that will be the end of your troubles."

That day came about nine months after Bob bought him. Willy's previous owner told me she never rode him out of an arena because he scared her. She said the one time she tried to ride around town, he spooked at things all the way down the road, so she went back home. Then she tried to take him on a mountain ride. They got about halfway up the North Fork trail when Willy decided to gallop down the mountainside straight to the horse trailer, jumping rocks and brush on his way down. It's a steep ride, even if you follow the trail. She never took him outside an arena after that.

When I first started riding Willy, he would spook at stuff in our corral. Bob told me he was faking and wasn't really scared. As usual, he was right. There were few things Willy was actually afraid of.

One day when no one else was home, I decided to take Willy for a ride around town. Clinton was quite a rural town back then. There were more fields than houses, and there was plenty of space to ride in the dirt alongside the road. I put on my English saddle, moon boots, and fluffy coat. I took along a bat whip because Bob told me not to ride Willy without one. I rode him up on the dirt road that ran along the railroad tracks east of our place. When we approached the first stop sign, Willy stared at the sign like it was a monster, planted his front feet, and snorted.

I didn't believe him. He tried to spin around, but I pulled him back to face the sign and swatted him with that little dinky bat whip (a bat whip is a short stick with a leather popper on the end; it's built for making noise). It was clear within a couple of minutes that I didn't have the right equipment. He knew he had me. I would have to scramble to stay on when he'd jump sideways or spin around since I had on the English saddle. Bob called them "self-dump saddles" since there isn't much to hold onto.

Kicking him was useless with those cushy warm moon boots on, and the bat whip felt like a love tap to him. I gave up after a few minutes and headed home. Willy bounced all the way there, pleased with himself. I was so mad at him that I literally saw red.

When we got home, I put on the Longhorn saddle. It was a western saddle with big swells and a high cantle, meaning it kept you in the seat. I put on cowboy boots, spurs, and traded the bat whip for a quirt, and we went back to the stop sign.

Sure enough, when we got there, Willy pretended it was a monster, and the fight was on. When I think back on it, I was lucky Willy wasn't mean, not really. He was a spoiled brat with no manners. He had needed a good spanking for years. It would not have done any good for Bob to spank him. The horse was smart enough to know who he had to mind and who he didn't.

Twenty minutes later, Willy had lost two shoes running backwards and spinning around, and I had an audience. I thought the people would be upset at me. I'd get him straightened around, and we'd head for that sign, and he'd throw another hissy fit, flat refusing to go past it.

Finally, after he ran backwards fast enough to lose that second shoe, he paused, breathing hard, and I kicked him forward. He walked as calm as could be, head down, reins slack, right past the stop sign without even looking at it.

The half-dozen people who had gathered to watch the fight cheered. They even clapped. I was too embarrassed to speak.

I rode Willy around town at least a couple of times a week after that. He liked to go places, and he didn't play tricks on me nearly as much in an arena, either. I think he had been bored to tears going around endlessly in those arenas and was glad to see new things.

He taught me a lot. I learned how to read a horse's expression so I would know when to call their bluff and when they were really scared. I learned that persistence pays, and I learned that sometimes we don't know what we want until we get it, even horses. Willy was a happy horse after that little episode.

He only tried one more trick on me. This was after we moved to Willard. I was riding him up on the canal road. Back then, there were cattle guards across the road, although most of the fences connected to them had fallen down or been removed. It was our second trip up there, and we came to the first cattle guard. Willy hadn't wanted to go out that day, and he figured the cattle guard was a good opportunity to spook. He snorted at it and spun around. I accidentally grabbed the wrong rein to pull his head around, and he ended up spinning a full circle.

He took off in a flat-out run, jumping the "scary" cattle guard and running pell-mell along the canal. He thought he'd spun around toward home. He ran for more than a half mile, jumping other cattle guards on the way, and I almost couldn't keep my seat in the saddle, I was laughing so hard.

Finally, he came down to a trot and stopped, looking around, confused. We were almost to Perry City by then. It was a pure accident he hadn't run home with me, but he must have figured I planned it that way. He threw in the towel that day and never gave riders trouble after that.

DUKE

The first two horses I started (that's horse-speak for being the first one to teach them to be ridden) were BJ and Buddy. After that, some of Bob's friends began hiring me to train their colts. Duke was the first horse I trained for someone else. Duke was a half-brother to Cutty Sark. I'd gotten to know Cutty Sark well by then, and I assumed Duke would be like her. In appearance, they were almost twins. Duke had the same sire as Cutty and Holy Smoke, too. The two mares must have gotten their brains from their mother, or Duke was simply born deficient, because he was not very smart.

He was the perfect horse for me to learn how to train on. I would have been lost without Bob's help. Duke needed every little step spelled out if you were teaching him something new. But once he got it, he never forgot. He ended up being an excellent 4-H horse for kids to ride. He didn't come up with his own ideas, so anyone could ride him. He was talented and athletic and ran barrels and poles the same way every time, and he was fast enough to bring in good times.

I'd ridden him about three weeks, and we were going along the side of the road when out of the blue, he decided to buck. There wasn't anything around that would have spooked him; he just took it in his head to try it. He didn't buck very hard, so he didn't dump me. I jerked his head around, growled at him, then kicked him in the side for good measure. He stopped bucking and stood there with an "Oh, that's what happens when I buck" look on his face. Then he walked on down the road and never bucked again.

Bob showed me each step to take to teach Duke things, and the horse was a blessing. Almost by accident, I learned what things a horse needs to learn first, and in what order. And Duke, even if he was slow to learn new things, was patient and kindhearted. He was as good a teacher in a different way than Willy and Tonto had been.

HOTSHOT

Sometimes you don't know what you have until it's gone. Things were simply easy for Hotshot. We ran him on the chariots when he was two, and we ran him around the hook on the flat track when he was three. "Around the hook" means Quarter Horse races that are long enough to go around the bend. Most Quarter Horse races are truly a quarter mile, hence the name of the breed. But some horses need a little more space to run well, and Hotshot was one of those. During his short racing career, he was always in the top four, even the one time the jockey lost his reins, and the finish line picture shows it looped almost to Hotshot's knees.

Willy liked to jump jumps even when he wasn't being ridden, and Hotshot started following him over. I waited impatiently until he was old enough that jumping with a rider wouldn't hurt his legs. When he turned four, I started teaching him to jump and began showing him at English shows in hunter/jumper classes and at horse trials (a.k.a. eventing).

Eventing is composed of three parts: dressage, which is in an arena with a specific pattern where you and the horse are judged on the quality of each maneuver; stadium jumping, which is a set of jumps in an arena where the only points against you are not meeting the time, and knocking poles down; and last is cross-country, which is solid jumps that are ridden out in the open. Hotshot loved all of it!

In fact, training him was too easy. He was the first horse I taught to jump and do dressage. He caught on to it all with ease. He knew on his own how to change his stride to meet the jump right, and dressage wasn't even a challenge. I moved him up in dressage and went to a few regular dressage shows because he soon got bored with the easier tests asked of horses in eventing competitions.

I didn't realize the gifts that were innately his until we sold him. The girl who bought him was the junior hunter/jumper champion in Utah that first year she showed him. It wasn't until I tried teaching other horses to jump and perform dressage that I realized what talent Hotshot had.

Hotshot was a lot like Willy in personality. He enjoyed his own "spook of the day." I rode the horses up on the hill and around town to keep them interested and in shape. He would pick something to spook at, just for fun. One day, it would be black garbage cans; the next, he would ignore those and spook at car windows, or maybe house windows (he'd even whinny at the horse in the window). Another day it might be mailboxes, and so on.

He also liked to eat trees. Willard is known for the fruit orchards that dot the hills. The summer before I sold him, we were riding along the canal road, and Hotshot snagged a branch off a tree that was full of cherries. He happily munched away while I rode down off the canal and into town. It was a Saturday afternoon, and there were many people out and about working on their yards or enjoying the nice summer afternoon. I waved at the people, and instead of waving back like they usually did, they scowled at me. When I got home and dismounted, I saw Hotshot's mouth was stained red from cherry juice.

I've always regretted selling Hotshot, although he had a good life with the girl who bought him. Since then, I've never ridden a horse who simply understood how to move to get the job done as well as he did.

YOU'RE MARRYING HER

If you're going to own a stud horse, you have to be willing to stand up to them and win arguments. They are always trying to be boss. It's in their nature to vie for the top spot—always. One day, our studhorse Patches had escaped and run down the road to try to find a way into a pasture with some mares in it. Luckily, the pasture had a good fence, and he didn't get in. I walked down there with a lead rope and halter and eventually caught him.

It was about a half mile back to the barn I was renting, and I didn't want to walk back, so I hopped on bareback and we headed home.

Bob and Robert were standing by Patches' corral, watching us head their way. It was June, the month before Robert and I got married. I rode through the alfalfa field, and when I came to the edge, we encountered the cement irrigation ditch.

Patches had not wanted to come along and fussed all the way, jigging and tossing his head. He thought the ditch was a good opportunity to see if he could throw me off. He snorted like he thought the tiny ditch was scary and spun around. He threw in a sideways buck when he did and bunched up to run. I jerked his head around, kicked him in the side, slid off before he could throw me off, and led him back to the ditch.

When we got there, he tried to jerk the lead rope out of my hands and pinned his ears at me. Ears pinned flat back is serious business in the horse world. It is a challenge for dominance. If you ever let a stallion get away with that, you'd better do something about it, or you're going to get hurt. I took the end of the lead rope and started whaling on him so he'd back off.

It only took about a minute for Patches to throw in the towel, but while I was chasing him backwards and growling, I heard Bob say to Robert, in a wry tone, "You're marrying her."

DIFFERENT IS JUST DIFFERENT

Horse people can be quite opinionated about *everything* to do with horses and often tend to be loyal to a certain breed. Bob's favorite breed of horse was the American Quarter Horse. He's not alone in that opinion. Quarter Horses are the most popular breed by far worldwide.

There is something to be said about loyalty. It's a good thing to be passionate about the things you love. I like the looks of a good, stout Quarter Horse. I like their muscle and their good minds. Those are generalities, though. There are a *lot* of Quarter Horses, and the breed has its own bad apples. But when it comes to looks, the build of a good stock horse is my favorite. However, when someone asks what breed I like best to ride, that's a different story. My answer is, "What will I be doing with the horse?" They always give me a "Huh?" look, so I explain.

Horses are bred for certain things the same way dogs are. Quarter Horses are bred for quick speed, which makes them handy for all sorts of things like working with cattle and running barrels and poles. An all-around useful horse, in general. But to excel at a certain task, it most often depends on the breed of horse. It's their conformation that matters. Are they built to do the job you want them to do?

There is nothing that compares to a Thoroughbred for jumping cross-country. They literally *float* over jumps with their long sloping shoulders, sleek muscles, and broad flat hocks. On the other hand, if you want a horse to pull a heavy load and not run off like a ninny at the slightest thing, you get a draft horse that has a calm mind, straight shoulder, big round muscles, and cow hocks.

When I was training horses full time, I was a woman in the horse trainer world, and a lot of men were intimidated by that. Horse training was supposed to be their territory. They didn't like me butting in. After showing at a few Quarter Horse shows, I decided I'd rather get into showing Paint horses. Bob called the Paint horses Holsteins, which is the name of a big, slow, spotted dairy cow breed. He'd say things like "You bringing home another Holstein?" when I'd unload a Paint horse.

When I started training horses in that big red arena, people brought horses to me in every shape, size, and breed. I soon learned that there are good horses in every breed, and bad ones, too. There are those with talent and brains, talent and no brains, and neither of both. It was quite a rough education, horses being large and dangerous, and I loved nearly all of it, even the long hours and low pay. The most frustrating thing was there were few people who could help me, and those who could rarely would.

These days, trainers have figured out if they educate the people along with the horses, they can prosper even more than if they keep their training secrets to themselves. I was about twenty years too early for that trend, though. Eventually, I figured things out with a lot of help from Bob and found that starting colts was my favorite thing. The problem was, the people needed as much education as the horses, and few would admit to that. Especially if they had an older horse with issues. Like Willy, most horses soon figure out who they have to mind and who they don't. I could fix their horse for them, but it wouldn't last unless the people were willing to take some training too.

After nearly seven years of training horses full time, the man I rented the arena from sold it. The new owners were not good to get along with, so I got a "normal" job and mostly gave lessons after that, usually to 4-H kids. Then I could spend time with horses for fun instead of as a job. It turned out well.

After leaving the red arena, I would take horses from time to time to train, and many years later, for a couple of summers, I trained some Paso Fino horses. I found them fun to work with.

They are small and shuffle along in a gait that, if they are bred correctly, does not bounce no matter how fast they go, and they can shuffle along *really* fast. Sheep move in a shuffle like that. When Bob heard I would be training some Paso Finos, he said, "Don't let those cowboys see you riding a sheep." Yep, he liked a good, solid Quarter Horse.

But they were fun little horses, made for riding fast across country. They don't feel small when you ride them. I saw a t-shirt once that said, "Paso Fino—the ultimate four-wheeler." It's true. They go up mountains just like a dirt bike without the noise. I enjoyed them very much for the short time I worked with them.

Besides liking various breeds of horses, depending on the job at hand, I also enjoy various disciplines or types of horse events: Western, English, and Driving. What's that old saying? "Jack of all trades, master at none." I tend to like variety a little too much. When I hang around the English riding people, I hear complaints about how the Western people do things. They'll say things like, "They harrow the arenas too deep, it's hard on a horse's legs." Or I'll hear Western people say, "There's no reason to ride with a noseband" (called a cavesson in English lingo).

The thing is, there are valid reasons for both. It's dangerous to ride a barrel or poles pattern at speed without a deeply harrowed arena; dangerous for both the horse and rider since the horse can easily slip and fall. But if you want to practice jumping or dressage, it's much easier on the horse's legs if the arena is not deeply harrowed. On an English bridle, there is no chin strap to keep the bit from sliding out of the horse's mouth, hence the need for a cavesson.

There are other endless debates and finger-pointing among horse people about whether to use shoes or not, how to longe a horse, how to load a horse into a trailer, how tight to have the bridle. The arguments go on and on. I've become more of a middle ground person as I've gotten older.

There has been a revolution of sorts in the horse industry. Trainers have found that sharing their knowledge with the people, not just the horses, helps everyone. They also use psychology rather than force and repetition to train horses, and everyone has benefitted by it. It's not really a new way of doing things. True horsemen have always trained horses that way. They just didn't share their knowledge.

If you're a horse person, before passing judgment when you see someone doing things in a way you would not, ask yourself why. Or better yet, ask them why they're doing things that way. Politely, of course. Who knows? You might learn something. On the other hand, you might find out something you *don't* want to do. It's all knowledge you can store away.

Different is just different; it doesn't mean it's wrong.

PART THREE:
FARM CRITTERS

PERSPECTIVE

We all rely on our own experiences to interpret the stories we're told and the things people say. Sometimes our own view is quite different from others. Some examples come to mind immediately. The first was when I was employed in Ogden, Utah, coding and editing tax returns. I was in my early twenties, and it was the first job I had that was full time indoors. We sat at sets of tables put together in pods. There were twelve people in each pod. I was busy writing the little red codes on the returns when another person in my pod piped up and said, "Why would a farmer have fourteen limousines to sell?!"

I looked around at the others in the pod. The rest of them were all city people. Everyone had comments about that. The most prevalent was that they wished they made enough money to have fourteen limousines. It took me a minute or so to figure out they meant cars.

I said, "A *Limousin* is a breed of cow. The farmer is claiming cows, not cars."

They all blinked at me, dumbfounded, and then we all busted up laughing at the same time.

Personal perspective plays other roles, as well. Rivers and mountains, for instance. When I was training horses at the big red arena in Willard, a lady named Becki came to me for some English riding lessons. She was from Alabama and was staying in Utah for a year. One day, I suggested we ride up the hill instead of doing a lesson in the arena. She had mentioned before that she had rarely been on trail rides. There weren't places near where she learned to ride in Alabama where you were able to do that.

Behind the arena was a long gravel road that led up the hill to the canal. The canal provides irrigation water for the farms below and runs from Ogden all the way to Brigham City. We stopped to give the horses a breather when we got to the canal. The canal isn't far up the hill, but it is a fairly steep road to get to it.

From behind me, Becki said, "This isn't a hill, it's a mountain." She sounded quite concerned. "How do we get down?"

I looked back at her and saw she was looking with trepidation over the brow of the canal road at the steep hillside. I laughed and said, "It's okay, horses go down almost as easily as they go up. It's not a problem."

I had already teased her more than once about the tale she told of the first night she and her husband got to Utah. It was after dark as they drove from the airport, and they both commented on the "pretty white clouds." When they got up in the morning, they realized those clouds were snow on the mountains.

We ended up being the best of friends. She got me back for laughing at her discomfort at the ride up the hill when I went to visit her in Alabama a couple of years later.

We were out on a "lake" waterskiing and fishing. We'd been out there all morning. I was sitting in the water with the skis out in front of my face, waiting for them to putt out to get the rope taut. I caught movement out of the corner of my eye and glanced over my shoulder. Through a break in the trees, I saw a massive barge with stacks of storage containers on it. Beyond that, on the other side of that vast expanse of water, concrete pillars, unmistakably those of a nuclear power plant, rose up into the blue sky. We were far enough away that the pillars looked small.

Sounding a little panicked, in fact sounding a lot like Becki had on the canal road, I shouted, "Where *are* we?!"

Becki's husband, Jonathan, shouted back, "We're in a side channel of the Tennessee River."

"What? This isn't a lake?" Where we had been all morning was as wide as Bear Lake back home, and they blithely called it a "side channel."

They just started laughing. Then another thought struck me as

I floated in the deep water, hanging onto the ski rope. "How big are the fish in here?" Yep, there was true panic in my voice that time.

Well, they really busted up then. When they got done laughing, Jon's friend pushed the throttle forward and they pulled me onto the skis. In only moments, I fell flat on my face and rolled over in the water, waiting helplessly for some giant fish to come bite me. I decided I was done waterskiing for the day and crawled back into the boat. I found out the Tennessee River was a mile wide at that point, and that was just the main river. The "side channel" was big enough to have its own name, although I cannot remember the name of it now.

A lot of the everyday words we use take on a different light if you're from somewhere else, especially if you come from east of the Rockies. Out here, our rivers are only creeks, our lakes small ponds, our gullies canyons, and our hills mountains.

And if you're from the country, limousines are cows.

***

On any horse ranch, there are more critters than horses. You'll find barn cats for sure, maybe a goat or two, plus a couple—or three, or four—dogs. These are some stories about the critters we had around the barn.

THE BANTY ROOSTER

Attitude matters more than size. That's true with animals, too. The best barrel horse I ever rode was a tiny sorrel mare. I had to wear knee guards on every run because she was little enough to slide my knee along the barrel all the way around.

But the turkey and the banty took the prize. I had a little Sebright banty rooster (a "banty" is a miniature chicken). He was maybe eight inches tall at most and probably weighed less than three pounds. My mom had a big brown turkey who would weigh in at around thirty pounds, ten times the size of the banty.

The banty spent his whole day chasing the turkey around. He only came up to the turkey's knee, and he'd go over and shuffle the tiny spurs on his legs against the turkey's leg, which was bigger around than that banty's whole head. Or he'd fly up and shuffle his little spurs on the turkey's head and then fall back to earth. The turkey would get all flustered and try to run, but he was too fat to go far. It was endless entertainment for us.

If video cameras had been handy back then, I know I would have made money on *America's Funniest Home Videos*.

GRODY GOAT

Grody as a youngster.

Bob's friend Vern had a passel of kids—five or six of them, anyway—and when I was training his little brown filly, they were all small. They decided I needed a mascot for the barn, so they gave me a gray pygmy goat. He was a tiny thing when they first brought him to me, barely weaned. Bob called him Grody, and the name stuck.

Grody was so small he could trot right through the wooden slats in the barn gate and escape onto our back lawn. The slats were about a hand width apart. To teach him to stick with me, I put a collar and leash on him and tied the leash to my belt as I went around doing barn stuff. He lived in an empty stall when I wasn't at the barn.

I'd had him about two months, and he had figured out to stay in the barn area when I was around, so he could wander by himself without being tied to me. One day, I was out cleaning stalls and needed to go to the house for something. I had barely gone in the door when the sound of Grody screaming had me running back out. If you've never heard a baby goat, they sound just like a little kid. Even when they bleat, it sounds like "Maaa!" No wonder baby goats are called "kids."

Anyway, Grody was stuck in the gate. His belly had gotten wide enough that he couldn't get through the slats anymore. He was screaming bloody murder and trying to wriggle through. I went over and pushed him back in, and after that, he had the run of the barnyard.

Grody had quite the personality. He thought it was entertaining to scare new people. He would sneak up behind them and bite their butt or stand on his hind legs and threaten to butt them with his horns. When we would go out of town, we would ask our friend Danny to feed and water the horses for us, and Grody would bite him every time. He never once bit any of us, though. What's that old saying? Something like "never bite the hand that feeds you . . ."

Those little pygmy goats just get wider and wider until their bellies are about as wide as they are tall. People always thought Grody was pregnant. He had been "fixed," so he didn't stink like most billy goats. By the way, a neutered goat is called a wether. I have no idea where that word came from.

GRODY VS. PATCHES

The fence was only one of the times that Grody's belly got him into trouble. He grew to weigh about sixty pounds, and probably fifty-five of it was belly. The rest was horns. We had brought our studhorse Patches over from the arena to breed our mares. We turned him loose in our barnyard on his first day there.

Goats are smart, and Grody was no exception. He had gotten into the habit of waiting for us to grain the three mares and the foals that we were keeping in the barnyard. We fed them in mangers hanging on the fence. Once we walked away, Grody would go stand under their necks, raise up on his hind legs, and thump them under the chin. They would move away, and Grody would steal a bite or two of grain.

In the horse world, stallions are often not the boss. It's the lead mare who runs the herd, and stallions are there to guard the others, keep them in their herd, and chase any usurping males away. Even in a domestic herd, it's often a more determined and clever gelding, or a boss mare, that runs the show. Not the stallion. As a consequence, the mares wasted no time showing Patches who was boss when we brought him over from the arena that day, and he had to wait to eat at the last manger.

Grody stole some grain from the other three and then sidled over next to Patches, who ignored him. Until Grody chucked him under the chin. Without missing a beat, Patches grabbed a mouthful of the skin on Grody's back and threw him high into the air and across the barnyard. The fat goat flew at least twenty feet and landed on his side.

Bob and I were standing by the barn, watching all that happen. We stared in awe as the goat sailed through the air. We were shocked the horse could even pick Grody up, much less throw him so far. I was sure Grody would explode when he came back to earth since he was so fat, but there was absolutely nothing we could do about it.

Grody landed with a loud thud that sent a cloud of dust into the air. He didn't have time to contemplate his survival and regroup, though. Patches had followed him across the corral with his ears back flat and murder on his face. With more agility than I had seen Grody demonstrate since he was a tiny thing, he hopped up and started running. His mouth was open wide enough that his teeth were showing, and his tongue was sticking straight out. I was sure he was trying to holler, but no sound was coming out. Landing had knocked the air out of him, and there was no time for him to catch his breath.

Now that we knew Grody would live, Bob and I couldn't breathe either, for laughing. Goats are very agile, and when Patches got almost close enough to take a chunk out of him, Grody would dodge, change direction, and they'd be off again. Poor old Grody never did get enough air to make a sound; he just kept his mouth open in a silent, desperate bleat.

Finally, Grody thought of running toward us. Patches stopped chasing him when he ran behind Bob and me. He was a very humble goat for a while. Even the mares weren't bothered by him for a week or so. As you can imagine, Grody never bothered Patches again.

SAVE YOURSELF

That same summer, I was babysitting my niece and nephew in the mornings. Karlee was three years old. She was a lithe little kid with wispy blonde hair who was cheerful and busy, rarely holding still. She loved the barn critters and always wanted to be out with them. Grody and the horses were free to wander the corral during the day. For safety reasons, I didn't want her out there with them and the goat if I wasn't around, and I was constantly telling her to stay out of the barnyard. It was Grody I was more concerned about than the horses. He liked to butt people for fun, and he weighed at least as much as Karlee. I kept threatening her with Grody, saying he would get her if she tried going to the barn without me.

Ask anyone, and they'll tell you that the Hollingsworth side of our family is stubborn. I know I am, and Karlee was at times, too. She could play at the barn, and Grody would ignore her when I was around, so she thought I was fibbing about Grody "getting" her. I thought I was, too.

I was cleaning up our breakfast dishes in the house one morning and heard Karlee's cry for help. She had a squeaky little kid voice normally, so the fact that I could hear her holler all the way in the house was significant. Being an ambitious and curious kid, Karlee had more than her share of accidents when she was small and had recently been stitched up from another escapade.

I tore the door open and looked toward the sound. Karlee was clinging to the top of the big wooden gate. She wasn't able to undo the lock, so she attempted to climb into the corral by going over the fence.

Every time she would begin to move, either over toward the back yard or into the corral, Grody would slam the gate with his heavy horns and make it sway.

Being the stubborn Hollingsworth that I am, I said, "I told you not to go to the barn," and left her on top of that gate to figure out how to rescue herself. I went back into the house to finish the dishes. When I got into the house, Bob asked me what was going on, and I told him. He was furious with me for leaving the "baby" on the gate and went out and rescued her.

Karlee has never forgotten that day. I think it scarred her for life. But it did keep her out of the barnyard. She never ventured out there by herself after that. Many years later, I was lamenting leaving her there, and she said, "The best way to learn is trial by fire."

DAMN GOAT

When Grody got older, he liked to play with people for fun. If a stranger came into the barnyard, he would trot over to them and stand on his hind legs, challenging them to a fight. His horns were thick and wide. They curled over and almost touched his neck.

Sometimes, people would take the bait and grab his horns for a pushing match, especially the big burly horsemen who frequented our barn to talk racehorses with Bob. For a little pygmy goat, Grody was incredibly strong. Goats are made for pushing with their horns and hitting things with them. Even a sixty-pound goat could hold his own pushing against a grown man and will frequently win.

Grody also liked to sneak up behind strangers and bite them on the bottom. He was clever about it, too. He knew when people were watching and would pretend he wasn't paying attention to them. As soon as they were distracted or caught in a heated discussion, he'd walk behind them and grab a mouthful of pants and hide.

He started to get quite a reputation, and we found that visitors to the barn had already been warned about Grody. They would keep a wary eye on him, even if he had never bitten them in the past.

Bob would often enlist the help of his good friend Danny to help us haul hay, fix something at the barn, or do chores for us if we were away. Grody could always catch Danny unaware. He would either butt him when he bent over or bite his bum when he had his hands full. Needless to say, Danny didn't like Grody very much.

One time when we were on a horse trip somewhere and Danny was feeding critters for us, he had quite the day. First, he needed to pick up some things from the barn, so he shut the horses in and backed his truck into the corral. He was loading stuff up and heard a weird noise. He went to check out what it was. Grody was rubbing his horns against Danny's truck door. Maybe he thought they'd look better with blue paint on them. Danny chased him off with a stick, which didn't do much good because goats think chasing them is a challenge to fight. They aren't intimidated by it.

Grody bided his time until Danny pulled his truck out of the corral and came back in to feed. Danny let the horses out and lifted about half a hay bale in his arms to put the hay in the three mangers. Since his arms were full, Grody took the opportunity to bite him on the bum. Well, Danny couldn't do anything about it without dropping something except attempt a feeble kick at Grody. The second time he got bit, he did drop the hay while trying to kick the goat.

Then he picked the hay back up and headed for the mangers. After dumping the hay in them, he grabbed the rope off the horse walker and tried nailing Grody with it, but the goat was too agile and smart for that. Danny gave up after a few minutes. Winded, he went over to fill the water trough. He waited for it to fill, still holding the rope and keeping a wary eye on Grody. Grody had moved over by the horses to steal their grain and hay leaves.

Danny assumed Grody had forgotten about tormenting him and bent over to get some hay and other litter out of the water trough. Grody butted him in the bum and made Danny dunk his face in the cold water. His hat came off and got a soaking, too.

Danny started cussing at Grody loud enough for all the neighbors to hear. He glared at the goat, trying to come up with a way to get back at Grody without spooking the horses since he was over by them again.

The mangers we put the hay in were made from barrels with one side cut out and bars welded at an angle to hold the hay in. The horses would reach their nose through the bars to pull the hay out. One of the barrels had a bar missing. Horses like to shake their mangers to make the hay leaves fall—they like those best. The mangers would fall off the fence occasionally due to the horses constantly rattling them.

Sis, Mom's buckskin mare, was shaking her manger, and Grody hopped up so his front feet landed in the bottom of the barrel. The manger came off the fence and fell over Sis's head since she was eating at the manger with the missing bar. Now the barrel was hanging in front of Sis like a huge necklace, and her head was sticking out the top of the barrel. She wasn't happy about it. Sis spun around, snorting and blowing, and spooked the other two mares and foals. They all began running around the corral.

Grody ran over to Danny for protection. When "things go to pot" (another phrase of Mom's), the goat knew it was safest where the people were. Danny was too worried about the horses to care about the goat anymore.

It was several minutes before the horses settled down enough for Danny to get close and help Sis out. It took him a while to lift it off her head without her snorting and taking off. Eventually, both he and the horses came through it unscathed.

When we got home, Danny wasted no time telling us his story. Of course, in his version, there were more expletives than words when speaking of that "damn goat!"

GRODY DEPARTS

There's more than one reason why goats are dehorned when they're little. We discovered our mistake when Grody was about six years old. Grody had always been fairly pleasant to be around and didn't bother Bob or me with his biting and butting, so we didn't mind him. He was entertaining to have around. But when he turned six, he started to get ornery. He took it into his head to disassemble the barn. He would butt things for something to do. First, he started on the regular doors that led to the tack sheds. He smacked those until they were cracked and hanging off the hinges.

Then he started on the stall doors. They didn't have ordinary hinges. They were heavy-duty strap metal welded to the doorframes. The doors themselves were made from two-by-sixes set into angle iron. Grody would slam those regularly, I suppose because he didn't have another goat to fight with. I don't really know why destroying the barn got into his head. He would keep at a door until the hinges cracked, then he'd move on to the next one.

He took out three stall doors before Bob put his foot down and said Grody had to go. Bob asked around town, and the fire chief said he wanted a goat to eat the weeds around his place. It was then that I discovered Grody had quite the reputation around town. The fire chief backed his truck up right to the gate and had a big cage in the back of his truck. From his manner when he came into the barnyard, it was clear he had been told Grody was mean.

Grody followed me up to the man's truck, friendly as could be, and jumped into the back of the truck to get the grain I set there. We talked about Grody, and I explained that he liked people a lot, but he also liked to break things. The fire chief was glad to find out this was a goat his kids could pet and not avoid. I don't know for sure how long they kept Grody, but I did stop and pet him when we would ride up in the east part of town. He seemed content.

TEQUILA

Not long before Mom married Bob, he traded a case of beer for a donkey named Tequila. Tequila had to have been old already since he was totally white with thick hair that stayed thick even in the summer. He was a smart old boy; he could open any gate handle and could even figure out chains with snaps on them like Tonto. Bob was working swing shift at Hill Air Force Base in Clearfield, Utah, so he didn't get home until about two in the morning. When he got home, he'd pull into the driveway and make a beeline for the barn to feed the critters. If he dawdled at all, Tequila would bray.

A donkey's bray is quite loud and carries a long way. As soon as Tequila heard Bob's truck approaching, he would start to "pump up." Donkeys wheeze air in and out for a minute or two so they can get a good lungful, then they bray. It does not make you very popular with the neighbors when the ornery donkey wakes them up at two in the morning.

When we owned Tequila, we lived in Clinton and had a few racehorses and also broodmares. Bob would feed the horses their hay and grain, then head for the house to get some shuteye. Tequila would wait in the pasture for Bob to get in the house and close the door, then he would open his gate and go around to each stall and open their doors. The silly horses would run out, and Tequila would go in and finish their grain. He even knew who had the most food and would let them out last so he could get more grain to eat. He never let Pale Face Annie out, though—she hated him, and he must have thought it was too much effort to run away from her.

Needless to say, Tequila was fat. So fat, in fact, he had bumps on his back, and it was totally flat on top, so hay and dirt would get trapped there. He loved you to scratch his back and would follow you around until you did. He was too old and stiff to scratch his back himself.

On Sundays (it always seemed to be only on Sundays), he would open the gate between the house and the pasture, pass by our yard and the next two houses with perfectly good lawns, and go eat on the church lawn. Eventually, someone at church would discover he was out there and recruit a couple of the little deacons to take care of it. They would ring our front doorbell with Tequila in tow, often with a scarf or tie as a lead rope, and ask, "Is this your donkey?" I've always wondered how the old donkey could tell which day of the week it was.

Bob got tired of Tequila letting the horses out all the time. We tried all sorts of things to fool him, short of padlocks. Finally, Bob gave up on fooling Tequila and asked his Uncle Doug if he wanted to take the old donkey. Doug said he would. Donkeys make great guard "dogs" because, unlike horses, they will fight things instead of running away. There were always coyote problems out in the wild country Doug had a grazing permit for. Coyotes will kill the baby calves. So Doug took Tequila down on the desert with his cows. He raised a few Longhorns and regular beef cattle each year. His permit for cattle grazing was down on the desert near Horseshoe Canyon. They loaded Tequila up in the cattle truck and dropped him off down there with the cows to spend the winter.

When Doug came back that spring to pick up the cows, he ran into some park rangers in charge of the Hans Flat Ranger Station. The park rangers always wanted to talk to Bob and Doug since they knew the history of the area and had fun stories to tell, so they invariably dropped by to chat. Bob's dad, June, had raised cattle and tamed wild horses in the area for years. At the top of Horseshoe Canyon is a perfect plateau to corral horses. There are steep cliffs that form a big circle like a large round corral, and a narrow strip where you can drive the horses in then put up a gate to keep them there. June had put a pipe in the spring that always flowed at the bottom of Horseshoe Canyon and pumped the water up to the plateau and into a trough for the wild horses to drink.

When the rangers discovered Doug had arrived, they came by to talk, and eventually they asked, "Hey, do you know who dropped a tame donkey off down here? If we don't stop and pet him, he blocks the road and kicks our truck."

Luckily, Doug hadn't loaded any cows or Tequila in the trailer yet. He pretended surprise and said, "No, I have no idea where a tame donkey might have come from."

Tequila went back and forth with Doug's cows for a couple of years. Doug always made sure there were no rangers nearby when he loaded Tequila. In the third year, he couldn't find the old donkey and figured age had finally done him in.

Years later, we hauled our horses down there for a ride into Horseshoe Canyon, and one of the park rangers regaled us with his stories about the tame donkey someone dropped off. We found out he would not only kick their truck if they didn't pet him but would get into any stuff they left around the ranger station. He had even gotten into their storage shed more than once. We laughed along with the rangers and felt a little guilty, but we never did confess.

THE HAND TOWEL

We had a black barn cat named Midnight (I know, it's quite original as a name, isn't it?) when Jennifer was about two. He started out as a house cat, but when he began shredding the carpets, he was evicted from the house and taken to the barn to live there.

Robert and I were working on the barn fences. We were building them out of welded pipe in an effort to keep Clyde in— he laughed at lesser fences. Robert was welding the hitch rail on the south side of the barn. We were not finished building the tack room either, so there was always construction stuff lying around. The tack room did have a brand-new door, but one wall wasn't finished, it was only framed in.

Jennifer was occupying herself at the barn. Even the barn walls were still only a shell, so I could see her wandering as we worked. As I handed pipe and welding rods to Robert, I could see her come out and gaze our way. She would stare at us, then look at her hands with a worried expression, then she would go back into the barn. Finally, I thought I should check on what she was up to.

It turned out she had found a bottle of heavy-duty construction glue and painted the new tack room door with it, using her hands as the brush (the door still has the glue on it). Then, she tried to wipe the glue off her hands using Midnight. When I got there, her hands, shirt, and pants were adorned with glue and covered in black cat hair.

I couldn't breathe for laughing, especially at the expression on Midnight's face. He was highly affronted. Anyone who has owned cats will tell you they are vain. How dare Jennifer ruin his glossy black coat!

I was able to wash the glue off her hands but gave up on the clothes and threw them away. The glue on the door seemed impervious even to a chisel. I left it there rather than gouge holes in the door. Midnight was not so lucky. He didn't cooperate with the bath idea, so he lived with his hair sticking up at odd angles for a couple of months before all that hair with glue on it shed off.

THE BACK WARMER

Jennifer had a cat named Michael. He was a long-haired barn cat the color of a Siamese. He thought his job was to be the horses' back warmer. He would lie on any horse's back and settle in for a nap if they would let him. Misty, the gray Arabian I boarded, liked it best. She was getting fairly old by then, and the warm cat probably felt good on her tired back.

The problem was Michael would try it with *any* horse. He would lurk in the loft or on a fence and wait for a horse to get close enough for him to leap onto them.

Well, *cougars* leap onto horses in order to *eat* them. Most horses won't stand still for such things. Maybe Michael liked the crazy ride he sometimes got as much as he did the high, mobile, warm perch they provided when he got his way.

He would pick inconvenient times to try it. Like when the shoer was trimming hooves. He was not popular with our shoers (in our part of the country, farriers are called shoers).

Most of the time, Michael would pick a horse that was half asleep to try landing on and had spooked all of them out of a good nap more than once.

Clyde got him back one day. Occasionally, Clyde would let Michael go for a ride, but he wasn't averse to playing tricks, either. Michael had spent a few times riding around on Clyde or lying peacefully on Clyde's wide back while they both napped. So, the cat couldn't know Clyde was plotting anything. Their partnership had gone on for about a month. I was cleaning up things at the barn and generally puttering around. Clyde was standing next to the water trough with his head hanging over the fence rail, apparently napping.

Michael climbed up onto the pipe rail and sidled over toward Clyde. The cat turned and began quivering, tail twitching, his eyes intent on Clyde's back, ready to leap. Clyde was standing at an angle to the fence. His head was closest, but his shoulder wasn't too far off for the cat to make the leap.

Clyde didn't move, didn't give any sign he had even noticed the cat. Michael committed himself to the jump and launched out into the air. Clyde shifted sideways, didn't even move his feet, and the cat sailed under his neck and landed in the water trough with a splash.

Once again, I would swear Clyde was laughing when the cat, looking like a drowned rat with his long hair hanging down, scrambled out of the trough and dashed away.

CACTUS AND THE GERBIL

If you ask them, most people will say that a cat is smarter than a mouse. They've obviously never met Cactus. Cactus was not the brightest bulb. He was a big yellow housecat we had. He adopted my husband one day when Robert was visiting his friend Brian. A stray yellow cat that had been hanging around for a few days kept jumping into Robert's truck, so he brought him home.

Jennifer had a gerbil that she kept in a glass fish tank. She had put things in the tank to occupy the gerbil. His favorite spot was a little rock she placed in the cage. The gerbil would climb up on the rock and sit there to eat his food.

Jennifer talked her dad into letting her keep the new cat in the house. When Cactus discovered the gerbil in the cage, he decided he should catch it for dinner. First, he tried the wire mesh on top, but Jennifer taped it down with duct tape, and he gave up trying to get that off. Cactus spent a lot of time sitting on the wire top, staring down into the tank.

A little while later, Jennifer rearranged her room and put the gerbil tank on the dresser across from her bed. Cactus spent hours sitting at the end of her bed watching the gerbil. Every so often, when the gerbil would get close to the side of the tank, Cactus would leap at it and hit the tank, flattening his face like those cartoon characters do, and fall to the floor.

Well, at first, this startled the gerbil quite a lot. But after a few days when nothing happened to him, he stopped worrying. He would get a handful of food and go to his rock. He would sit on his little perch, facing Jennifer's bed, and wait. Sure enough, Cactus would eventually show up and make a leap for the tank.

We could hear the thump when Cactus hit the tank, even from the living room. The gerbil wouldn't even twitch; he'd stop eating long enough to watch the cat smash his face into the glass and fall, then go on eating.

DE DE AND THE
MONSTER MOUSE

My sister and her husband had to move out of the house they were renting into another place where they were not allowed to have pets. They asked if their two dogs could come live at our house, and we agreed to the arrangement. De De was a Great Dane. Sweetie was half short-haired Saint Bernard and half Basset Hound (drunk teenagers at a party were the cause of that mating). Anyway, they were city dogs. They were used to living indoors, were always on a leash when outside, and only went to the park to play.

Moving to the country was quite a shock for them. We are lucky in that our lane is more than six hundred feet from the highway, and there are acres of fields west of us. Our dogs are usually free to roam around outside. De De and Sweetie spent the first week keeping us awake at night while they licked their sore paws. They weren't used to all that running around.

De De was tall and regal, as her breed is. Not long after she came to live with us, I was out at the barn with a couple of the 4-H kids. Jasmine and Karlee were teenagers, and Jennifer was with us too. I went into the barn to get a can of grain and saw a tiny, half-grown mouse in the grain. I scooped up the mouse in the can and took it out in front of the barn. I hollered at the dogs to come and tossed the little mouse out onto the grass. Jack, our yellow lab, and De De were the only two out of the house.

De De was the first one to get there. Being a city dog, she had never seen a mouse. She sniffed the little thing, and it reared on its hind legs so that it stood about two inches high. De De pricked her ears and stared at the thing. She wasn't sure what to do, so she gently reached out a paw (it was five times the size of the mouse) and touched it.

It bit her.

De De jumped backwards, surprise and shock clear on her face. The brave little mouse started hopping toward her. De De ran backwards from it, even crashing into my legs trying to get away from the scary critter.

The girls and I couldn't breathe at that point.

Jack noticed something was going on. I have to digress here for a moment and explain about Jack. She was bred to be a seeing-eye dog, and she was blind (that right there is pretty ironic, and funny, too). She went blind from congenital cataracts before she was one year old. Apparently, that's a common problem in some families of yellow Labradors. We considered putting her down since it's dangerous around a farm for any dog, much less a blind one. But Jennifer's first word was Jack, so we kept her. As you can tell, Jack was a girl. Robert preferred female dogs, and he named them after football players. Jack's full name was Jack Lambert, linebacker for the Pittsburgh Steelers.

Jack got along great at our place and lived to be thirteen. The horses left her alone, even those who hated dogs. She knew where the path was clear and would run in those spots, and if we happened to be in her lane, she'd take out our knees or knock Jennifer flat when she was small. That happened at least once a week. You'd think we'd learn, but no. She could count the steps from the sidewalk to the front door and followed Jennifer wherever she went.

On that day, Jack realized something was up and began to circle around, sniffing the ground while De De stared in horror and scrambled away from the monster mouse. The little thing kept hopping at the giant dog.

Jack's circles got smaller and smaller until she zeroed in on the mouse. She ate it in one gulp. The look on De De's face was priceless: "Oh, that's what you do with it?"

SWEETIE TO THE RESCUE

Sweetie and Jack.

Since I mentioned Sweetie, I have a story to tell about her, too. Sweetie weighed nearly a hundred pounds, and her legs were short, so her belly almost dragged the ground. Her face and coloring were like a Saint Bernard. The rest of her shape was Basset Hound. Everyone who saw her seemed compelled to smile. Maybe that's why she was so friendly.

A couple of months after she was brought to our place, we decided we couldn't keep her. She was smart and liked to chase chickens, which made her very unpopular with Robert. Luckily, she wasn't very fast since her legs were too short, and the chickens would usually get away. But on the same week we decided she had to go, she earned herself a spot at our place for life.

Jennifer was still small. I think she was three years old. Robert and I were in the garage working on something, and Jennifer was in the back yard. It wasn't a lawn yet, just weeds almost as tall as she was. We could see her through the open back door.

Most Labradors are sweet, but the neighbor's dog that lived north of us across the fence was not. The fence only had three strands of sagging barbed wire since we hadn't put a new one in yet.

Out of the blue, that big black dog came rushing across the yard straight at Jennifer. We were too far away to do anything. My heart stopped. I was sure she was about to be mauled, if not killed. Sweetie came from nowhere. We didn't even know she was in the back yard. She hit that dog from the side right when he was leaping for Jennifer's face.

Not only did Sweetie clean the other dog's clock—when he turned tail, she followed him across our yard, through his yard, and up the stairs to their deck. The dog ducked into their house, and Sweetie followed him in. Then she stopped and ate the food from his bowl right in their kitchen.

The dog never set foot on our place again, and Jennifer never did learn to be scared of dogs, for which I am eternally grateful.

Robert proclaimed that day that Sweetie had a home at our place for as long as she lived. She lived to be seventeen. When she hit her teens, the vet declared her to be immortal. Neither Basset Hounds nor Saint Bernards are supposed to live that long.

POLAR BEAR!

Andy.

Did you ever watch those old cartoons with the sheepdog and the wolf? The sheepdog would lie around doing nothing until the clock went off, then he'd go to work guarding the sheep while the wolf tried to get a meal. I didn't know those cartoons were based on reality until we owned Andy.

Andy was an Akbash dog (which translates into big white sheepdog). They're a breed from Turkey. She was named after Anthony Muñoz, offensive tackle for the Cincinnati Bengals. She took her job seriously, although she didn't guard sheep—she guarded Robert's chickens. She would nap all day, lying around the yard, until dusk came. Then she would go down to the coops to patrol all night. She took it as a personal insult if a varmint got into the coops. She often treed coons, and if she caught them, she shook them until they died. She even learned how to catch skunks without getting sprayed. Yet she would let little chicks climb all over her, and hens shared her warm dog house.

She guarded us, too. If someone came to the house, she would sit quietly and unobtrusively about fifty feet away at an angle between us and whoever had shown up. She never acted aggressively, but I have no doubt if someone had threatened me or the girls, she would have taken them on.

There was one time when Robert shaved his beard, and when Andy spotted him coming through the gate at the coops, she went for the stranger. He ran around a coop to keep her away, yelling, "Andy, it's me!" She finally stopped barking long enough to hear him, then looked at him like, "Oh, hi, what have you done to your face?" Then she came over, tail wagging, to get a pet.

Another evening right after dark, we heard sirens, and one cop even came down our lane. Robert was friends with the local cops and went out to see what was up. A convicted felon, who was known to be armed, had run from the cops and was seen running right through our barn alleyway.

Robert was a former corrections officer. He got out his shotgun and stood on the porch, watching the cop cars. While he stood there, he could hear our neighbors ratcheting their shotguns, too. It's not a good idea for criminals to try hiding out in farm country.

A little while later, we saw a highway patrolman's car go down Fred's lane. He was shining a spotlight around the fields and spotted our buildings at the chicken coops. He drove his car right across Fred's alfalfa field and got out of his car, flashlight in hand. We could see Andy's white coat, even from up at our house. But she was careful not to stand where the cop could see her. She watched him approach, making no noise.

The cop put a hand on the fence that divides our place from Fred's, intending to climb over. Andy jumped out from where she was hiding and barked at him. Andy weighed about 175 pounds, so her bark was loud and deep, and in the dark, that white dog looked huge.

Cop and flashlight turned around and hustled back to the car. Robert heard the story from the Willard cop a little later. The patrolman asked him, "Who the hell keeps polar bears?"

BRUCE

When Robert and I were newlyweds, I had a little yellow Toyota truck with a camper shell on the back that I ran around in. The back window had been broken out of the camper shell, and I hadn't bothered to get it fixed yet. There was often hay and other farm things in the back. One afternoon, I got in my truck at work, ready to head home, and looked in the rearview mirror. There was a large dog in the back.

I got out and looked through the open back window at him. He was big, mostly brown with black points and a little bit of white. I couldn't place what breed he was. I guessed maybe part hound and part shepherd.

He wasn't very friendly and would not come to the back of the truck for me to touch him, so I left him in there and drove home, hoping he would not try to jump out. When I got home, I looked at him through the broken window. He didn't seem mean, and I could see he had been scuffed up and needed some help. I opened the tailgate and crawled in. He let me put a leash on him and hopped out of the truck. He had some road rash spots here and there but otherwise seemed to be okay.

Someone had taught him more manners than most dogs have because he walked at heel and sat properly when I stopped.

Our dogs were happy to meet a new dog, and he wasn't aggressive toward them. He wasn't friendly, either. Mostly, he seemed confused.

I figured he'd fallen out of someone's truck or been hit a glancing blow by a car. I put ointment on his sores. None of them were serious, and he was a little friendlier toward me after that. I offered him some food and water, but he wouldn't touch either of those.

Once he seemed comfortable, I checked his collar. There was only one tag on it, and all it had engraved on it was DL&L and a phone number. I called the number, and the woman who answered said in a crisp, business-like voice, "Deseret Land and Livestock."

I was a little taken aback at finding a receptionist on the other end of the line, not a dog owner. Deseret Land and Livestock is a huge company. I explained that I had found a dog in the back of my truck and brought him home to Willard with me. She asked why I was calling this number. I said it was on the tag. She seemed quite bored and disinterested. I gave her our phone number and address and figured we might end up with an extra dog at our place.

About a half hour after that, Robert came home, and I explained about the strange dog. He got along well with dogs, and it only took him a few minutes to talk the dog into eating something and drinking the water we set out.

I had to leave to meet some people at the barn who wanted to look over a horse we had for sale. I was away for a couple of hours. When I got back, the dog was gone, and Robert had quite the tale to tell.

About an hour after I left, a small truck that was quite similar to my little Toyota pulled alongside the house. It had a wooden pen in the back instead of a camper shell. The kind used to transport sheep. A tall, thin man got out of the truck and peered at the house. Robert opened the door to ask the stranger who he was. The new dog was standing beside him, so he hooked a finger in his collar to keep the dog from leaving when he opened the door.

As soon as the tall man spotted the dog, his face split into a huge grin. He opened his arms wide and said, "Bruce!"

The dog was very happy to see his owner. When we talked to the dog, he would look at us with a puzzled expression, like he couldn't quite understand us. It turned out that his owner had a very thick New Zealand accent.

Bruce was a Huntaway. Although I had never heard of them before, they are a popular breed in New Zealand and Australia, used for herding sheep at great distances. The shepherds will stand on a hilltop and direct the dogs with whistles. Deseret Land and Livestock (DL&L) had paid $10,000 to buy Bruce and ship him over from New Zealand. He was supposed to be their new stud dog. They had only had him a couple of weeks.

That morning, they put him in that same small truck with the sheep pen in it to haul him and a couple of the female dogs up to the vet on 12th Street, which was the same street the building I worked in was on. When the man got to the vet's place, no Bruce. He had climbed out. Maybe the female dogs were too much for him.

My truck must have smelled like home since it had hay in it and looked like his owner's truck, so Bruce hopped in.

DL&L had even used their helicopter to fly up and down 12th Street that day, looking for him. Needless to say, his owner was a very happy man to find Bruce. Bruce rode in the front of the truck when they left, and two weeks after that episode, Robert received a thank-you card and a bottle of very nice scotch from Bruce's owner.

CITY DOG VISITS THE COUNTRY

Robert met Dave when they were corrections officers at the prison. They became good friends, and Dave brought his family to visit our place more than once when his kids were small. One day, he asked if he could bring his new dog Duke. He was a Rottweiler puppy that was about six months old. He was a large dog, and even half-grown he'd have weighed about eighty pounds.

He was very excited about the new sights and smells. Dave had quite the job keeping the heavy dog from pulling the leash out of his hands.

First, they went to the chicken coops. Duke spotted a hen with chicks and pulled Dave over that way so he could sniff them. The hen promptly shuffled the spurs on her feet across his face and down his side. He about knocked Dave over trying to back away from the scary hen.

A few minutes later, Dave and Robert decided to head back toward the house. When they went through the coop gate, Duke spotted the horses. He just *had* to go see what those giant things were. He lunged, barking his head off, and ripped the leash out of Dave's hand.

Unfortunately, the first horse he came to was Baraza. She hated dogs. A pack of them had run her through a fence when she was two, and she had a vendetta against dogs ever since. She went after Duke, teeth bared, and chased him to the gate up by the shop. He was so terrified that he missed the walk-through hole and ran into the gate at full tilt. He was watching that monster chasing him, not where he was going.

The mare called it good when the pup hit the fence, and she didn't stomp on him. Duke cowered against the gate until Dave and Robert caught up to him. They decided it would be safer if they brought him to the house.

Jack was sleeping in the spot of sunshine that was coming through the front door. When Duke came into the house, he sniffed at the strange dog. Jack came off the ground, snarling and snapping. She was normally sweet to other dogs, but this one had startled her out of her nap.

Duke backed away from the vicious dog and ran into our half-grown kitten, who promptly laid the end of his nose open with her claws.

He was a very humble pup after that and stayed right next to Dave. Poor thing had been traumatized. I think he was very glad to get back in Dave's truck and go home to the city life.

CHARMIN AND HARRY

Occasionally, Bob would pawn off some sort of critter, like one of his old racehorses, on his daughter Jessie. Every so often, she'd return the favor. She talked Mom into getting one of her little Shih Tzu puppies.

Jessie's house had a wall separating the kitchen from the living room, with an opening on each end. Mom tried out several names for the puppy on our way up, but none of them seemed to fit. She decided to wait until she met the pup to come up with a name.

When we walked in the door at Jessie's place, she was yelling at one of the pups. The pup had taken the toilet paper from the bathroom and had already made one lap around the kitchen/living room wall when we arrived. She did two more laps before anyone could catch her.

Mom said, "Charmin!" and the name stuck. Charmin seemed to know she belonged to Mom from the start. While we were visiting, Jessie talked Bob into taking a pup home for himself, too. That's how he ended up with Harry.

Charmin was exceptionally smart for a tiny dog, but when they were passing out brains in heaven, Harry forgot to get in line. After he grew up, one of our favorite pastimes was to catch Harry sleeping on the couch. If we said, "Harry! Come here!" and sounded really excited, he would hop up and run straight off the couch into midair.

It was just like one of those cartoons with the legs running in place and then the startled look when they realize there is no ground under them. Lucky for Harry, the couch wasn't very tall, but it was still enough for a good laugh.

Harry would often get lost. He couldn't find his way home even if he were a half-block away. Bob took him almost everywhere he went, and people in town got to know him. Harry standing on Bob's lap while he drove around town was a familiar sight. There was a cost to taking Harry with, though. He was constantly locking Bob out of his truck. He'd step on the button when he stared out the window if Bob left him there for even a few seconds.

More than once, Bob had to walk home, usually from one of the barns I rented. Harry always seemed to lock Bob out when there was no one around to give him a ride. Finally, Bob put one of those magnet key holders on his truck with a door key in it.

The crowning glory for Charmin and Harry was when they won the most creative float in the Willard 4th of July parade. Mom and Bob hooked the two dogs to my daughter's stroller and dressed the stroller up as a covered wagon for them to pull.

THE FULL MOON

Before we moved into our current house, Robert had his chicken coops at the end of the dirt lane that is now the drive to our place. My brother Den had recently moved into the old Barker house at the top of the lane on the highway. Robert went down to put the chickens away and discovered a skunk lurking around the coops. Skunks are literally death for chickens. They will wait for a chicken to stick their head out of the wire, then eat the head. They'll kill several chickens that way in one night. Plus, they're often infected with either distemper or rabies.

Robert drove to the house to get his gun, and on the way back, he pounded on Den's door to get him to come out and help him shoot the skunk. Den had been getting ready for bed, but he was game to go skunk hunting anytime. Den's boy D.J. was only about nine, and he didn't want to miss the chance to hunt a skunk either, so they both grabbed their guns and headed down the lane with Robert. By then it was dark, and a bright full moon was climbing into the night sky.

Since Den was getting ready for bed when Robert hollered, all he'd put on was what was closest to hand: swim trunks and flip flops. When they caught up to him, the skunk was heading west down the lane.

About the time they spotted it, they were barely within shotgun range. Den, being the one with the longest legs, was in front. He swung his shotgun up and started to aim—and his shorts fell down around his ankles. He hadn't taken the time to tighten the string on his shorts. As Robert liked to tell it, "It was a full moon above, and a full moon below."

At that same moment, the skunk turned around and came at them. It was on the fight. Den was holding his shotgun in the crook of his arm and reached down to try to pull his shorts up, but he couldn't get it done fast enough. The skunk got within range, spun around, and started spraying.

Den shuffled backwards with his shorts wrapped around his ankles and lost his flip flops because they aren't made for that kind of travel. His other hand was hanging onto the shotgun.

Robert and D.J. were no help at all. They couldn't even function, they were laughing so hard. Even if they could have brought their guns up to get the skunk, Den was between them and it on the narrow lane.

Den got skunked so bad that his wife, Debbie, wouldn't let him in the house. He had to clean up outside with the hose. They threw away the swim trunks and flip flops.

To this day, D.J. can't even tell the story. He starts laughing too much.

THE SLEEPER

Speaking of my brother, he is quite a heavy sleeper. This first became apparent when he was living in Ferron, Utah.

He had a dog named Space that was half red wolf and half husky. Space liked to chase cats, and he played with them like a cat would a mouse once he caught one. Needless to say, Space was not very popular with some of the neighbors who liked cats. He did leave the cats alone that belonged to the neighbors, but strays were fair game in his book.

One evening right before Den was turning in for the night, he saw Space had a huge black tomcat cornered, but since that was not unusual, he went inside to get ready for bed. A few minutes later, he heard a loud *boom*! He thought, "Dang, someone has shot Space!" He assumed the cat he'd seen had an owner after all.

He dashed to the front door and threw it open. Space was sitting on the neighbor's lawn across the street. The dog looked at Den as if to say, "What?"

Den shrugged his worries away and went to bed.

The next morning, Den stepped out of his front door, coffee cup in hand, and blinked at the sunrise. Thinking of nothing in particular, he looked across the road to his neighbor's house and could see someone stirring behind the curtains. Then his gaze wandered to his old red truck, which was parked in his driveway.

His eyes caught something unusual. There were tire tracks going crossways from the drive and ending in his front yard. When he looked closer, they were obviously large truck tracks, and there were a couple of other car-sized tracks, too. The neighbor's lawn had even more tire tracks on it.

While he was contemplating how curious that was, Space came trotting over to get a pet. He scratched the dog's ears. "Huh," he thought to himself, "that's odd." He followed the track of the tires, and they ended at the power pole that stood in the opposite corner of his neighbor's yard. There was a black lump at the edge of the road under the light pole.

Right about then, his neighbor came out the door. "Were you home last night?" he asked, sounding incredulous.

"Yeah, why?" Den asked.

"Man, you sleep like the dead! That damn dog of yours" (he added more words that aren't normally printed) "chased that huge stray tomcat up the power pole and shorted it out!" He pointed at the black lump. "The pole caught on fire, and we had fire trucks and cops and everyone on our front lawn!" His voice got louder as he spoke, and he added a few more expletives. "You really slept through all that?"

"Guess so," Den shrugged.

The power company had only left a half hour earlier from putting in a new power pole. The fire burned the top of the pole off and dropped the power lines onto his neighbor's front lawn, so they'd spent all night repairing lines and drilling a new hole for the pole.

No one had moved the cat.

About then, Debbie came out on the front porch holding her own coffee cup. Den wasn't the only one who could sleep through an earthquake.

That wasn't the only time they snored on through a ton of noise and commotion. When we were still living in the tiny house that we rented before our house was built, we got a call from Bob to come help round up Fred's dairy cows. They had broken out and were wandering around Den's house.

Robert and I threw clothes on—it was about midnight; critters always seem to pick the middle of the night to escape—and took off for Den's place. The herd was quite excited to be out and kept mooing to each other and trotting in a circle around Den's house. There were at least thirty of them, so they made quite a racket. To add to the noise, Bob, Fred, and his dad, Don, were bellowing orders. Robert was the loudest of all and added some colorful curse words to the mix. When we would pass Den's bedroom window, Robert would pound on it, but to no avail. Den and Debbie and their two small kids slept through the whole thing and had no idea what happened until they came outside the next morning and saw cow tracks and cow pies all around their house.

SKUNK

Thinking of skunks reminded me of another story. There are those people who, when the shit hits the fan (one of my mom's favorite phrases) jump into action and take care of things. They are rarer than the other kind. Most people simply freeze.

When I was in my late teens, I had a job as an exercise rider for racehorses. Trainers like to take them out early, so it was about six in the morning. The filly's owner wanted to gate school her, so we put her in the gates. She was very nervous and kept moving. You don't want to open the gates until they stand, so we had been in there too long for her liking. She was scared anyway, and the gates are just too enclosed, and they make strange noises. The filly couldn't go forward with the gate in the way, but she felt she had to go somewhere, so she jumped up. When they do that in the gates, they usually flip over backwards.

Luckily, our friend Clyde was the header, and he kept a good enough hold on her bridle so that she didn't go all the way over. She did, however, flip me hard enough backwards that when my helmet hit the back of the gate, it tore the leather straps off it. There were half a dozen men behind the gates, and Clyde was the only one who got moving when things went bad. He reached over and jerked me out of there before the horse could squish me any more than she already had.

At first, I thought all I'd come away with was a few bruises. I slept most of that day away and then thought I was okay. It was a couple of weeks before I realized there was more wrong than that. When I tipped my head back, I would get dizzy. Finally, I went to get X-rays. It turned out my neck bones were straight—they're supposed to have a curve in them, and the nerves in my neck were being pinched. If something had hit the top of my head with even a little force, it would have severed my spine.

That was the end of my job galloping racehorses. It took a few months for a chiropractor to get my neck bones in the right shape again. It also took me a while to realize that I had lost my sense of smell. It's sort of an invisible problem and can be rather inconvenient. Like when the wall heater in the tiny house we lived in on the highway had a gas leak. I had been getting headaches for a couple of weeks and couldn't pinpoint why. My chair was right in front of the heater. Robert was a smoker, so his sense of smell was not too great either. My sister came to visit, took one step in the door, and said, "You have a gas leak."

I also think my family often fibs to me when they say dinner tastes good. After all, I can't tell one flavor from another. The only things I can taste are sweet, sour, bitter, and salt. I do remember what things tasted like, but if my eyes were closed, I doubt I could tell you what I was eating if the texture didn't give it away.

It's probably why I get along so well with critters, too.

The lack of a sense of smell lends itself to some humorous moments. My husband claims it's the reason we stayed married since I couldn't tell if he smelled bad.

I can't tell if dogs smell bad, either. Our old English Mastiff, Gene (named after Gene Upshaw, lineman for the Oakland Raiders), was known to clear a room when she cut loose with a fart, and I'm oblivious.

But my greatest fear when it comes to no sense of smell came true a few years ago. I had always worried about the dogs getting skunked and me letting them in the house. Skunks are a frequent hazard when you live in the country and own dumb dogs.

One night at four in the morning, Gene insisted on going out, so I let her out the door and waited for her to bark to come back in. Luckily, when I let her in, she went straight over to Robert's side of the bed. He woke out of a sound sleep and exclaimed, "What reeks?"

Yep, she'd been skunked. I promptly put her back outside.

263

Then I found we didn't have the ingredients in the house to wash her with, so I drove to Walmart and got them. If you don't know the recipe, it's one part baking soda, one part hydrogen peroxide, and a little bit of dish soap. You need a *lot* of hydrogen peroxide and baking soda for a dog the size of Gene. It works well if the smell hasn't settled in. At least that's what they tell me when I'm done washing the dogs and our clothes. Maybe they're lying?

BUCKING BULLS

One thing that both city people and country people will agree on is that bucking bulls are cool to look at. They're not exactly pretty. Even when a person says, "That's a pretty bull," they mean cool. But city people often don't have an accurate perspective about animals—not what they're really like since they haven't had the opportunity to live around them. They must go on assumptions and with what the TV shows portray, which paint a skewed picture of reality.

Animals have their own opinions about what they should do, and the larger they are, the more spectacular it becomes when they have a difference of opinion about things. Rodeo bulls are no exception. Some of them are tame and cooperative. Others not so much.

For instance, Robert's friend, who I will name Sam, was a partner in the Broken Heart Rodeo Company. He was asked to provide three bucking bulls for a commercial the Ford company wanted to film.

The director had a vision. Picture this: the wide expanse of white sand and salt that makes up the Bonneville Salt Flats in northwestern Utah. Three new shiny Ford pickups are arrayed on the flats. A magnificent bull comes striding through the trucks, portraying strength, power, invincibility. It would be awesome!

The director came out to the ranch to choose the bulls. He picked a massive brindle that was half Brahma and had their characteristic hump behind the neck. The second was a huge spotted bull with impressive stickers (that's rodeo-speak for long horns that stick out). And the third bull the director wanted was bigger still. He was a deep red bull with banana horns (they curve down instead of up). When the director pointed to that one, Sam said, "You don't really want him. How about that one over there?" He was thinking, "of course he'd pick the orneriest bull on the place."

The director insisted on those three, so Sam agreed. After all, they were going to pay him a lot of money for not a lot of work, so he didn't argue. He spent a couple of weeks training the bulls by parking some old trucks in a field and then placing the cattle trailer at the far end. One of the cowboys would let the bulls out of their pen one at a time on the other side of the pasture. Sam would stand by the trailer and shake a can of grain. It worked great! The bulls would mosey through the trucks and then up into the trailer to get the grain. They loaded up and headed for the salt flats.

The first two bulls were perfect. They did exactly what the director wanted. They walked casually through the trucks, pausing every so often as cattle do since they're rarely in a hurry, but on film, it would appear as if they were pausing to admire the trucks. The bulls were looking at the trucks just because they hadn't seen them before, but it didn't matter. The director's vision was realized.

After the second bull performed so well, Sam tried to talk the director out of using the third bull, since they already had some good film. He kept the banana bull for last, hoping the first two would satisfy them. He figured they already pushed their luck as far as they should that day.

The director was not to be dissuaded. He insisted on filming the third bull, too. Sam sighed. He and the cowboy who had come with him exchanged knowing looks and shook their heads but carried on. Sam took his place near the cattle trailer then signaled to the cowboy at the bullpen to let the last one out. Things began okay, and for a moment, Sam dared to think they might get away with this.

The bull came out of the pen, ambled slowly through the trucks, and even tossed his head for effect. The director was practically giddy things were going so well. From his post at the trailer, Sam could hear the man gushing about how great this idea was, and how wonderful this commercial was going to look.

Halfway through the trucks, the bull paused. Sam shook the can of grain a little desperately, hoping against hope the bull would come join the other two. The bull looked at him and considered the grain and the trailer for a moment, but he didn't move that way. He flipped one ear backwards, raised his nose, and bellowed. The director went into paroxysms of joy. How majestic the bull looked with his head up like that!

Sam paled. He'd seen the look in that bull's eye. If you're around critters, it isn't long before you can read what's on their mind. And the look that bull gave Sam when he considered the trailer meant he did not intend to come quietly. As my husband put it when he recounted the story, the bull clearly flipped them the bird.

You know those big white shade things the movie industry uses to make the light just right for the cameras? That was the bull's first target. Then he went after the film crew.

The salt flats are truly flat; you can even see the curve of the Earth there since it's so wide and featureless. Needless to say, there isn't any cover. Their only option was to abandon their equipment and take shelter inside their vans.

From there, they had a good vantage point. They watched helplessly while that bull destroyed thousands of dollars' worth of cameras and equipment. Not a single camera was spared. No piece of film could be saved.

Once the entire scene was trashed, the bull stood in the middle of the wreckage and huffed a couple of times. Then he quietly walked up to the trailer and got in.

His work there was done.

JEFFREY

I first learned that hummingbirds are ornery and tough when we lived in the tiny house on the highway. There was a huge old trumpet vine right next to the front door. There would be over a dozen hummingbirds around that vine every day when it was in bloom. There were more than enough flowers there for all of them, but they would spend most of their time fighting with each other over who got which flower.

When Jennifer was only seven or eight, we were at my mom's house helping put things away after the July 4th celebration. It had been very windy the night before, and we were picking up branches and lawn furniture that had been blown around.

While we were cleaning things up, Jennifer found a hummingbird nest on the driveway. She was examining it and saw something moving out of the corner of her eye. A tiny baby hummingbird was on the hood of Mom's car. It must have fallen there when the nest blew out of the tree. She scooped the little thing up and brought it to me.

She wanted to try to save it. I assured her it would die. Birds are so fragile, and this appeared to be the most fragile thing I'd ever seen.

We happened to have a cage with tiny mesh on it. My mom had kept button quail in it for a little while until Bob built a larger pen for them. We put the little thing in it, and Jennifer christened him Jeffrey.

Every couple of hours, she would hold an eyedropper for him to drink nectar out of. It was a good thing school was out because she didn't get any sleep the first week or so. Unbelievably, the little creature didn't even get sick. He was too tiny at first to fly, but he would hop around and keep himself busy. When he was hungry, he would squeak. It was amazing how loud such a little thing could be, and how tough.

Eventually, he grew flight feathers, and by August he could fly around in his cage. Jennifer would let him out, and he would zoom around the house, then stop and sit on her finger. He would fly by the rest of us and hover right in front of our noses, but the only finger he would perch on was Jennifer's. By the time he could swoop around the house, he had his adult plumage, and we realized Jeffrey was a girl.

When she was obviously fully grown, I told Jennifer it was not right to keep her. Hummingbirds are not pets. They belong in the outdoors. Jennifer reluctantly agreed, so we took the hummingbird outside, and she flew up into the aspen trees in our front yard. We had hummingbird feeders hanging in the trees, and there were a couple of other hummingbirds buzzing around. Jeffrey sat in the tree and squawked loudly. She was hungry and was not happy that Jennifer wasn't feeding her. Then she spotted the other hummingbirds getting a drink and went down to try it out. In a minute or two, she had it figured out. When the other hummingbirds flew away, she went with them.

We assumed that was the end of it. But no. For three years, each spring, Jeffrey came back to visit. She would hover right in front of our faces to say hi, then buzz away with the other hummingbirds.

THE HOUSEGUEST

Before the first year I was married, if someone had asked me if I believed in ghosts, I would have probably shrugged and said, "I don't know, I've never really thought about it." That was before we lived as newlyweds in the old house in Willard.

It was a large, drafty stone house. It was one of the original houses built in Willard in the late 1800s. The ceilings were ten feet high, and the only heat was a huge old heater standing in the space in front of the stairs to the second floor between the spacious kitchen and the living room. I'm a lizard—I like it hot—so I was always freezing in that house. Robert, being an Eskimo in disguise, was perfectly content.

The first sign that something was odd was the small closet bar in the room next to the stairs. It was about two feet long and sat in normal little cups that closet bars are mounted in. It was not easy to put back in, so it wasn't like the bar was too short or came out easily. Every time we went to the house before we moved there and hung clothes on it, the bar would be on the floor.

We started renting the place in July, three weeks before we got married. Robert would crash there to sleep instead of driving all the way back to Salt Lake. We started moving our stuff in. Mom's house was on the same street, so I would just load my things into my little yellow pickup and bring them over.

The stairs that led to the second story were narrow, and each step was taller than normal since it was built before standard codes. The stairs turned a corner halfway up. Anytime I walked up them, they always felt chilly, no matter what temperature the rest of the house was.

The upstairs had three large bedrooms. One had a door going out onto nothing since the widow's walk balcony had long since rotted away. Occasionally, people passing by would see the curtain over that window move, and a shadow would cross in front of the window when no one was home.

There was only one bathroom. It had been added onto the west side of the house and attached to the kitchen. The laundry room was also an addition. Decades before we moved in, they had closed in the back porch and put the plumbing in there for the kitchen and washer. To the left of the kitchen door, opposite the washer and dryer, was the door to the cellar.

Once we moved in, we noticed that doors would be open that we knew we had closed, and lights would go on and off at random. We did have three rambunctious dogs, so it wasn't too farfetched to pin the weird things on the dogs' antics. But after a while, we had to admit there was more to it, especially since things often happened when the dogs were outside in their kennel or lying on the floor in plain sight.

Fat Cat, who was a kitten when we moved in, never seemed to notice anything. But the dogs did. We would be sitting in the living room watching TV and the dogs would jump up, the hair would stand up on their backs, and they would growl while their eyes tracked something going across the room. Robert and I never saw anything ourselves, but occasionally we could feel it.

There were cold pockets that seemed to follow me around. The house was always cool, even in summer, since the walls were about a foot thick and made of rock, with lath and plaster inside that. The window wells were deep enough I could set potted plants there. If I was doing things and suddenly turned around or went through a doorway, I would pass through a cooler spot.

One of the first things our guest did was throw Robert's large ceramic coffee mug onto the kitchen floor. It was his favorite one. His mom had made it for him. I had washed the dishes and remember leaning the coffee mug against the wall to dry on top of the dishes on the counter. When we heard the crash, we went to investigate and found the mug smashed in the middle of the floor about four feet from the kitchen counter.

Next, it knocked Robert's guns over. There were about a half dozen of them, a mix of shotguns and rifles, leaning against the wall in the corner of our bedroom. We didn't have the money for a gun safe yet. The dogs were outside that day. We both heard the crash. I was busy making dinner in the kitchen, so Robert went to check out the noise. Then he started shouting, cussing, and telling the ghost he was going to get a priest to exorcise it out of the place if it didn't leave his guns alone. It never did bother the guns after that.

The door to the middle bedroom upstairs was warped and would stick when you tried to open it. I'd have to tug until it popped open. It seemed that the ghost wanted that door halfway open and the lights on because that's how it always was when I went up there. The room only had Robert's hunting gear stored in it. I gave up eventually and left it like the ghost wanted.

We discovered that the more we seemed to notice what it did, the more it seemed to do. It was like our consciousness of it lent it energy.

My friend Becki and her husband were visiting one time, and I suggested she try out the huge claw-footed bathtub that was original to the house. I *loved* to soak in it. Becki gathered up her robe and toiletries and headed for the bathroom.

A few minutes after Becki went into the bathroom, we heard her yell. Robert and I were in the living room watching TV. It was Becki and Jon's first day at the place, and we hadn't mentioned the ghost yet.

She had filled the tub with hot water and went to turn it off, but the tap wouldn't work. Then it sprang a leak. When we got to the door, it was stuck. Robert had to jerk on it to open it. We had never had issues with that door before, or the bathroom plumbing. Water was spurting up from the tap. So much for my idea of Becki getting in a peaceful soak.

Another time, our friends Gayle and Troy were visiting. We had discussed the ghost earlier, and they scoffed at us, as most people did. We were used to the skeptical reactions we got by then. We had all settled in to watch a movie. There were two large octagon-shaped end tables next to the living room chairs. A stack of videotapes was on one of them. We were all absorbed in the movie when the stack of videotapes scattered across the floor. They didn't fall over; they flew out into the room like someone took their arm and swept them off.

Troy was poised to take a sip of his beer. His hand stopped in midair, and he said, "Did I see that?" They were both more inclined to believe our stories after that.

Lance and Brian were skeptics too. They were Robert's hunting and fishing buddies. Willard is close to some good duck hunting ground, so Robert told them they could stay at the house while we were away for the deer hunt. Jokingly, he said, "Don't disturb the ghost."

They laughed at him and ribbed him for believing in ghosts. They were sure we invented the stories just because the house was old and would be more believable. They came up on Friday night, hunted for a while, then crashed at our place. Their plan was to stay until Sunday afternoon. But very early on Saturday morning, they were at my mom's place with the key to the house. They never have told Robert what happened that Friday night, but both of them refused to stay at the house after that.

The ghost in the house was certainly odd, and a little unsettling, but there was only one time it truly scared me.

I was in the laundry room, standing at the dryer folding clothes. The washer and dryer were where the back porch had been. The room was about ten feet long, and the door to the cellar was at the opposite end of the room. There were three doors at that end: the cellar, the back door, and the kitchen door.

It was overcast that day, so the light was a little dim, but not enough that I had to turn the lights on. Suddenly, I felt an overwhelming sense of dread and menace. Slowly, I turned around.

I couldn't see anything, but I knew *exactly* where the thing was. It was blocking all three doors, and it was focused on me. Until that moment, I hadn't gotten a sense of it being a person, or maybe the leftover spirit of one. But at that moment, I knew that it was a woman, and she was *very* angry.

I stared at the spot for a long time. It was so silent in the room

273

that I could hear my heart pounding. I really wanted to escape, but to get out, I'd have to go through her. Finally, after several minutes, I couldn't stand it anymore. I dashed through the kitchen door as fast as I dared without actually running. Somehow, I felt that running would make me even more scared.

Right before I passed through the door, I hit a cold mist, like fog feels, even though it was a sultry summer day. I went out the kitchen door and hustled to my mom's place and stayed there until Robert came home.

After that, I started looking for other places to live.

One of the last things it did before we moved away was scare Robert. That wasn't an easy feat. He worked as a corrections officer in the maximum-security part of the prison when we were first married.

We were both working nights. When I drove down the road, I could see the house glowing. It looked like every light in the place was on. Curious, I went in the door and found him in the bedroom. He was lying in bed with his arms folded across his chest and his .45 Magnum in his hand.

I said, "Um, what's up?"

"We're moving," he said.

I blinked and said, "Okay, when?"

"Tomorrow!"

I looked at the stubborn set of his jaw, at his crossed arms, and then at the gun. "Uh, what happened?"

"The damn ghost flipped the breaker and . . ."

I just had to interrupt at that point. "You were going to shoot a ghost?" I snickered. Who says I'm not caring and sympathetic?

He narrowed his eyes at me while I tried not to laugh out loud. "I thought someone was in the house," he explained. It was clear he meant someone *not* invisible.

Then he told me his story.

He entered the house through the side door into the kitchen like always and headed for the cabinet to get a glass. When he opened the cupboard, he felt someone rush past him, slam the cellar door open, and pound down the wooden stairs. Then the lights went out.

Robert, sure he had spooked an intruder in the house, went to the closet and got his pistol and his Mag-Lite (the huge black flashlight cops carry around). Then he carefully made his way down the cellar stairs with the flashlight casting deep shadows beyond the beam of light. In the cellar, from which there was no escape, there was no one. He made his way to the breaker and flipped the lights back on.

There was nobody in the cellar, there was nobody in the house anywhere—he checked all the rooms, which was why all the lights were on when I got there. He finally decided it must have been the ghost.

We did move shortly after that, although it wasn't the next day. Luckily, the ghost stayed with the house. Others living there noticed the ghost, and others did not. I often wonder what it was doing there, and why it makes its presence known to some but not others.

Mostly, I'm glad it didn't follow us.

VACUUMING
CORPSES

The second year we were married, after the big ghost house, we moved into a tiny house on the highway. The house was made of brick, and the original part was twenty feet by thirty feet when measured from the outside. The bedroom had been added onto the back wall of the house. The ceiling in that room was too low for us to put the bed on a frame, so it was on the floor. As tiny as it was, I liked that house. It had personality.

We heard an odd scuffling, scratching, and sometimes a low hum in the wall behind the head of the bed for a couple of weeks. We both assumed it was mice or maybe birds sneaking into the space between the bricks and the added-on bedroom wall. We didn't bother to investigate.

Down the road, a quarter mile south of the tiny house, Robert and I bought the lower five acres of my brother's property from him. I was down there working on building the barn and came back for some lunch. Robert was already home in his chair, watching TV. I fixed a sandwich and then went to get something from the bedroom.

It was an overcast day with dark heavy clouds looming, promising rain, although it wasn't raining yet. The bedroom had no window, and one of us had left the light on when we got up that morning.

When I opened the door, the room was *full* of hornets. And I mean *full*. It wasn't a handful; it was dozens of them. I glanced at the bed, and Fat Cat was lying there sound asleep. Maybe she thought the hum was soothing. I carefully closed the door and went back into the tiny living room.

"Robert, the bedroom has hornets in it."

He didn't even look up when he said, "Well, the flyswatter is around here somewhere."

"No, I mean it's *full* of yellowjackets!"

A little annoyed at having to get up, he clomped to the bedroom and opened the door. He stood and blinked, dumbfounded by the swarm of hornets making the room hum. And at the stupid cat who opened one eye to glare at us, annoyed that we were disturbing her nap. He watched the hornets buzz around for several seconds then carefully closed the door again.

The hornets had come in through the holes in the light fixture. They were attracted by the bright light since it was so dark outside that day. It turned out their nest was in the wall between the bedroom and the main house. There was open space in the roof over the bedroom, and the light could be seen from there.

We went to get some cans of hornet spray. Robert spent a good five or ten minutes spraying those hornets in the bedroom. Then we went outside and looked for their nest. We found it on the north side in the space between the bedroom and the brick wall. I think the whole wall must have been a hive because when he started spraying, hornets swarmed out of the hole and began to pile up at the base of the wall. The mound was at least a foot high (that is not an exaggeration) by the time they stopped coming out.

A little while later, when I was cleaning up the bedroom, my mom called.

"What'cha doin'?" she asked.

"Vacuuming corpses."

THE GIFT

Like our houseguests, this last story isn't one about farm critters. It's about an unusual teacher. I hope everyone has at least one teacher who makes a big difference in their lives. Mr. Godfrey was my seventh-grade English teacher. I was a very unhappy kid at the time. Divorce is hard on kids, even if their parents are civil to each other like mine were. We had gone from living in a nice house on a corner lot, where all the neighbor kids gathered, to a tiny trailer. Due to the move, all of the kids I grew up with attended a different junior high. I had also lost many friends the year before when I refused to take sides in the heated and nasty school president campaign. Trying to be neutral didn't work—they all felt I was a traitor.

Church would normally have been a comfort, but shortly after I started attending the new ward, I discovered that the adults in charge of our ward were swapping wives. Disgusted, I wasn't about to listen to those hypocrites. My mom asked why I wasn't going anymore, so I told her. She didn't believe me until their infidelity was discovered about a month later by more than kids and the ward was disbanded.

Starting junior high, I was out of my element. New school, new crowd, and I was too shy (people who know me now won't believe that) to make new friends. So I didn't go. At that time, as long as you had a note from a parent and stayed away all day, they didn't count attendance against you. It was probably kids like me that changed that. I would take the city bus to Salt Lake and hang around with other truants there or wander the mall. I could get away with it because I looked older than I was. I was also expert at forging my mother's handwriting. I'd attend school enough to find out what tests were coming up and then show up for those, so the teachers were passing me along. All except Mr. Godfrey. He knew attendance was important.

He failed me the first quarter of seventh grade. It was the first F I had ever gotten. My mom called the school to find out what was up and discovered I was rarely there.

I don't know what would have become of me without Bob and the horses. Even teachers like Mr. Godfrey and special moms like mine can't fix things if you feel you are of no worth.

It's up to you to change you.

Mr. Godfrey was an inspirational man. He *cared* about his students as people, not their scores or his own career. It was important to him that we learned more in class than English.

I received an award from Weber State College for this story. It was what made me believe some people might be interested in the things I wanted to write about. This was the last of the stories I wrote for that biographical writing class I took when I first attended college. Although the scene in the lunchroom is slightly exaggerated (what storyteller doesn't embellish a little bit?), it is a true story.

If you think you have a good story or something important you want to share with others, just start typing.

MR. GODFREY: A CHARACTER SKETCH

The seventh-grade class sat nervously at their desks in the large gold-carpeted room. Everyone had the first day of school fidgets, made worse by the stories we had heard about this weird English teacher we were about to meet. Ten minutes dragged by, and still no sign of him. Just as we were all hoping we would get to delay this fateful meeting, in stormed a strange apparition. Tall and skinny, swinging a bamboo cane from his large thin hands, and moving with a feline grace that made the cane seem out of place. He wore jeans and a t-shirt. Our other teachers wore suits or skirts. The most shocking feature of all was his wild hair, a bright orange-red, sticking out all over like someone had plugged him into a light socket. His beard was a darker shade of orange and neatly combed. He would have looked like a clown except for his piercing blue eyes that, when they fixed on you, looked like they could see into the depths of your soul.

"Hello, I'm Mr. Godfrey." He scowled down at us over his long thin nose. We all began to sink behind our desks. Then he said, "No, too serious," and abruptly pulled himself out of the room with the cane hooked around his neck! An instant later, he was back, strolling in with a casual air about him and a mischievous grin lighting up his face.

"Hi," he began. "You can call me Mr. G or Mr. Godfrey, just so you don't forget the 'Mr.' One of my ancestors gave up and changed his name because Godfrey is what everybody said anyway when they saw this hair."

We all started to chuckle, he smiled, and we broke into gales of laughter as the tension drained away.

We soon found out that life with Mr. G would never be dull. He began our Honors English class with the basics, starting with spelling bees. But even those were not to be ordinary. Not only did we have to stand until we missed a word, but we had to keep up with him as he played tennis with his cane and a Nerf ball. If the ones sitting hit the ball back before the ones standing did, they could stand up and try spelling again. The last one up got to go to lunch with Mr. G in the cafeteria. At first, we thought lunch with a teacher wouldn't be such a wonderful treat, but Mr. G worshiped food. I guess he could get away with it since he was so incredibly skinny. He always brought his own food and would eat that, plus what they served at the school.

Mr. G would share the tasty pastries and exotic gourmet items he brought from home with the lucky winner. As they sat eating with heartless zeal, everyone else in the spacious lunchroom would stare over their tables, sniff the air, and covet the delectable treats. Somehow, regular lunch didn't seem nearly as appetizing.

After the first day of school, we never heard him get a student's name wrong. He knew us each as individuals and often knew other things we did with our lives. He would astound a student by commenting on what they were up to after school or over the weekend. When we'd ask how he could possibly know those things, he'd say, "Watch the world around you, pay attention to the little things people do. Take it all in!"

He quoted *Mame* constantly. "Life is a banquet, and most poor fools are starving to death!" Then he'd lecture us on "don't waste this gift of life." He would single out a student, lean forward on his cane, and scowl, asking, "Who are you? How would you define yourself? Think about it. If you know who you are, you'll be happy."

He was still an English teacher, even though he didn't always stay within that realm. We were given a syllabus in class at the beginning of the year, and we couldn't believe how much he expected from us. Later, most of us came to accept all the work because he never did ask for more than he gave. He wrote lists of book suggestions and somehow always knew if we had read the books we chose, even if he didn't assign an essay to turn in.

We were required to read *Romeo and Juliet*, and like most teenagers, we thought that was cruel and unusual punishment. Not only did he want that, he demanded that we memorize six hundred words from the play and repeat them to the class! But then we began our discussions on Shakespeare. We found we were about the same age as Romeo and Juliet, that they had a lot of the same problems as we did. They became real to us. The true meaning of tragedy became clear. It was no longer just a word to remember for a test. Then began a lengthy soul-searching to discover an alternative ending to the story. Each of us wrote a different ending than Shakespeare had. Imagine requesting seventh graders to rewrite a famous work!

After the Shakespeare sessions came talks about books and the messages in them. We were shown an infinite variety of thoughts included in their pages. We learned to read between the lines. *The Grapes of Wrath*, we were shown, was foreshadowed in chapter three of the book, a chapter that had seemed out of place before. It told of the turtle trying to cross the highway, which turned out to be a representation of life and the people who would try to run it over, or avoid it, or help it.

Mr. Godfrey spoke in a drab monotone, which was in contrast to his character. But when he read a book, he breathed life into it. The words came alive, no longer only letters on a page.

One day he bounced into the room, late as usual, and asked, "Who knows what Middle Earth is?" He didn't believe in slow beginnings. A few of us tentatively raised our hands. "Well, speak up, what is it?" he demanded.

"The age that Tolkien writes about," one girl ventured to say.

"Right," he grinned, but he wouldn't be satisfied with that. "Where is it?" He raised his orange eyebrows and shot an inquiring look around the room.

One boy was brave enough to say, "What do you mean, where is it? It's not real, it's in a book."

"Tolkien put it there, didn't he?" Mr. G responded. None dared say anything. "Then, if he wrote it, the book was in his head, right? And, if you read it, Middle Earth has now become a part of your life. A part of your memory."

He began to spin the worn cane and pace across the room. We knew from experience a lecture was coming. "Books," he began, "are a gift. Once you have read them, they're a part of you. You can put trash there, or you can put good things there. It's up to you. Remember this, not all gifts you'll be offered are good, but *you*"—he emphasized, throwing a steely glare at us and pointing his cane—"can decide whether to receive them or not."

Mr. G was intolerant of apathy. He would fly into a ten-minute tirade if some student said they didn't care or wouldn't try. We would all want to weep for the poor soul upon whom he vented his wrath. Nothing was worse to him than a quitter. "Never give up!" was another favorite phrase of his, and we all wondered if his consuming ambition to live life to the fullest had anything to do with the ever-present cane. We were never to know; he always sidestepped any questions we put to him about it.

A couple of times at lunch, Mr. G arrived without his usual gourmet repast. The first such instance was enough to cause every student who knew him to flock around his table to see what might become of this unusual event. He went on calmly eating and talking as if nothing were out of place in his routine. All of us noticed, however, that the other teachers who frequented the lunchroom had drifted to the edges of the gym, which doubled as the lunchroom, near a handy exit.

All of them except Mr. D the history teacher, who was Mr. Godfrey's good friend. He sat at the opposite end of the crowded room, attempting but failing to hide a grin. A few of us also noticed that the school's vice-principal was stationed close by. He threw threatening looks at Mr. G whenever he could catch his eye. This only caused Mr. Godfrey's mouth to turn up into a sly grin on the side of his face the vice-principal couldn't see.

Something was definitely going to happen. After a few minutes, the school secretary bustled in and asked the vice-principal if he would come to the office. Shortly after he left, an unsuspecting student walked over to talk to Mr. D, diverting his attention.

Suddenly, Mr. G jumped to his feet and yelled, "Food fight!" as loud as he could. He let fly with a spoonful of potatoes. They struck Mr. D's glasses as he turned too late to miss the inevitable blow. He wasn't caught flat-footed. He flipped cream peas back across the room. They sailed past Mr. G, trailing cream, and landed in the long blonde hair of the girl sitting behind him. She turned, without hesitating, and slung her carton of milk back across the room, not knowing who had thrown the peas, which now dropped innocently amid the growing mess on the floor. Food flew everywhere, along with trays and a few well-aimed spoons with particles of food still attached.

The melee ended abruptly when the loudspeaker broke into the din and the vice-principal's voice blared. "Anyone contributing to the disorder in the lunch hall"—he sounded like he was gritting his teeth—"will be severely reprimanded!"

Calm suddenly reigned. Only the sound of people whispering and the ping of dropped utensils could be heard. Slowly, those of us who had been near Mr. G crawled out from under the table. On a cue from him, we had all taken refuge there and came through virtually unscathed.

Everyone spent the next hour mopping floors and polishing tables, but none complained. We never did discover whether Mr. G was reprimanded, or if the vice-principal leaving had all been a plot of his.

Mr. Godfrey gave us all a unique view of "the journey of life," as he would say. None of us viewed English, books, and learning quite the same way after that year. To this day, spelling bees make me think of tennis, and lunchrooms make me smile.

A FINAL WORD

The goal Mom and I had when putting this book together was to compile the stories Bob and the rest of our family liked to tell, and to add some food for thought to the stories, too. Mostly, we wanted to give you at least one good belly laugh. We hope we succeeded.

ABOUT THE AUTHORS

R.E. Beebe lives on a small farm in Northern Utah. She has two beautiful daughters and lots of pets—the normal kind. She is the author of the paranormal fantasy series *Sylvio*. For more information, visit www.beebebiz.com.

J.M. Marsing was married to Bob for 33 years. She lives in Northern Utah also, a mile from her youngest daughter.

53773273R00171